DADDY GRACE

DADDY GRACE

An Annotated Bibliography

Compiled by
LENWOOD G. DAVIS

Bibliographies and Indexes in Afro-American
and African Studies, Number 28

Greenwood Press
New York • Westport, Connecticut • London

`Library of Congress Cataloging-in-Publication Data`

Davis, Lenwood G.
    Daddy Grace : an annotated bibliography / compiled by Lenwood G.
Davis.
        p.   cm.—(Bibliographies and indexes in Afro-American and
African studies, ISSN 0742-6925 ; no. 28)
    Includes index.
    ISBN 0-313-26504-6 (alk. paper)
    1. Grace, Daddy, 1882?-1960—Bibliography.   I. Title.
II. Series.
Z8364.D3   1992
[BX8777.6.Z8]
016.2899—dc20   91-42599

British Library Cataloguing in Publication Data is available.

Library of Congress Catalog Card Number: 91-42599
ISBN: 0-313-26504-6
ISSN: 0742-6925

First published in 1992

Greenwood Press, 88 Post Road West, Westport, CT 06881
An imprint of Greenwood Publishing Group, Inc.

Printed in the United States of America

♾™

The paper used in this book complies with the
Permanent Paper Standard issued by the National
Information Standards Organization (Z39.48-1984).

10 9 8 7 6 5 4 3 2 1

For

all of the members of the

UNITED HOUSE OF PRAYER FOR ALL PEOPLE

Contents

Introduction

Let me say from the outset that of the more than twenty bibliographies that I have compiled, this one has been the most difficult. The main reason why it was so difficult is that Bishop Charles "Sweet Daddy" Grace wrote very little and left few records. During his lifetime, the leader granted few interviews. A lot of what we know about Grace and his church comes from *The Grace Magazine*, the official organ of the United House of Prayer For All People. Unfortunately I have not been able to locate any back issues of the magazine. No copies were found in either of the two leading African American repositories on Black materials in the United States, Schomburg Center for Research in Black Culture or the Moorland-Springarn Research Center at Howard University.

Most of the major Black and White newspapers wrote very little about him. Moreover, when they did write about "Sweet Daddy" Grace, most of the comments were negative. Bishop Grace's organization, the United House of Prayer For All People, was very secretive. Unlike Father Divine and other cult leaders, few members of Grace's church left his organization and those that did leave did not comment or write about their defections.

Most of the things written about Daddy Grace have been nefarious, to say the least. He has been characterized as a phony, con man, fraud, an imposter, rip-off artist, charlatan, sinner, and a pretender. I do not know if he was all or any of those things. What I do know is that his followers believed him to be a man of God. Although many of his members contributed large sums of money to his movement, perhaps August Meier and Elliott Rudiwick best explain what his followers received in return for their contributions:

The dollars which Grace received from the poor who flocked to his services, and which made him a wealthy man, were for the people themselves a small price to pay for the void he filled in their lives.

Daddy Grace's movement was a form of escape from the drab and frustrating daily lives led by many of his followers. Don Oberdorfer summed up Daddy Grace's movement this way:

Members of the more orthodox churches may stand on the sidelines and sneer all they please, but the fact remains Bishop C. M. Grace had something to offer the humble people who gave him allegiance. And that obviously was something they could not get in any other denomination—respect and a sense of belonging.

Most people focus on the negative aspect of Bishop Grace. Dr. Alex Poinsett points out, however, that Grace did have some positive programs:

1. He established a pension fund for retired ministers and old, indigent members.

2. He provided a family association burial plan for his followers.

3. He built or bought, in every major town where a House of Prayer was located, multi-unit apartment buildings to house his church members.

4. In emergencies, he provided them with free food, clothing and shelter.

Perhaps Dr. Alex Poinsett best sums up the essence of Bishop Charles "Sweet Daddy" Grace by concluding that:

although Bishop Charles M. (Sweet Daddy) Grace departed before he could balance his material accounts, the world will do the final bookkeeping on his moral ledger. Others will say, with equal conviction, he was a colossal fraud. Only God can judge.

Although several versions have been given about Daddy Grace's birth, the general view is that he was born on the Cape Verde Islands off the coast of West Africa around 1882. Little is known of his parents or early childhood. Due to this lack of concrete information, certain details concerning Daddy Grace are hazy, and change from article to article about him. (One of the more obvious examples of this is Daddy Grace's middle name, which is sometimes said to be "Manuel" and sometimes said to be "Emmanuel.")

It appears that he came to the United States about 1901 and settled in New Bedford, Massachusetts. Before he founded his first church (mission) in 1919 or 1921 in West Wareham, Massachusetts, Grace found employment as a railroad short-order cook, sewing machine salesman, cranberry picker, proprietor of a grocery store, and a patent medicine salesman. Tradition has it that Grace built the first church himself out of "rocks" that no one else would use. He called his church the United House of Prayer For All People, Church of the Apostolic Faith.

In 1923 or 1924 Grace started a church in Charlotte, North Carolina, after holding services in a huge tent in that city. It seems that Grace incorporated his House of Prayer in 1927 and set up headquarters in Washington, DC. Grace had churches located in every major city from Florida to California and claimed over 4,000,000 members. He and/or his church had many business interests, including: apartment buildings, a soap factory, a coffee plantation, a chicken hatchery, a cosmetic company and a garment factory. When Charles Emmanuel Grace died in Los Angeles, California, on January 12, 1960, it was estimated that he and/or his church was worth $25,000,000, according to the *New York Times*. It was later discovered that his personal wealth was little over $100,000, according to the *Washington Post*. Grace always contended that he had no personal money and that he was only administering the church's money as its trustee.

This book, like any book, could not have been completed without the assistance of many individuals to whom I am most grateful. I am indebted to Kay M. Marlowe for typing the final draft of the manuscript and helping organize the book. I would also like to thank my daughter, Tatia M. Davis, for helping with the proofreading and giving some valuable suggestions. I am appreciative to Janice Harris for sharing with me information on the House of Prayer. Several librarians also assisted me: The Schomburg Center for Research in Black Culture; the Moorland-Spingarn Research Center at the Howard University; the Winston-Salem State University Library; the Wake Forest University Library; the University of North Carolina at Greensboro Library; and the Library of Congress. I would also like to acknowledge the assistance that I received from several newspapers. They are: *Standard-Times* (New Bedford, MA), *Charlotte* (NC) *Observer, Charlotte* (NC) *News, Washington* (DC) *Post,* and *Winston-Salem* (NC) *Journal-Sentinel.*

Although this is the only annotated bibliography on Daddy Grace, it is short because of the scarcity of materials on the subject. Hopefully, in the future more data on him will become available. I take full responsibility for any shortcomings that the book may have.

I
BOOKS

A. Background Information

1. **Blythe, Le Gette, and Charles Raven Brockman.** *Hornets' Nest: The Story of Charlotte and Mecklenburg County.* **Charlotte: McNally, 1961, pp. 214-216.**

This book observed that Daddy Grace's United House of Prayer For All People congregation in Charlotte occupies (in 1961) the largest single Black Church structure in the city. The writers believe that Grace started his church in Charlotte in 1924. The cult leader made it a custom to visit the Gate City each summer and had a home there. Some saw Grace as a repulsive charlatan and phony and others believed him to be a prophet. . . . In any case, a historical lesson can be learned and that is that the downtrodden, hopeless and rejected are always ripe for leadership, conclude the writers.

2. **Eaton, Hubert A.** *Every Man Should Try.* **Wilmington, NC: Bonaparte Press, 1984, p. 124.**

Hubert A. Eaton is a Black medical doctor from Wilmington, North Carolina who was seeking an elective seat on the local board of education in 1952. He recalls that he sought the support of Bishop C. M. "Daddy" Grace and the support of his church members. Dr. Eaton and some members of his campaign staff visited Daddy Grace at his home on South Seventh Street. When they went to his home, he was eating lunch and they were invited to join him. Dr. Eaton continued, "A girl in early adolescence stood near Daddy Grace and fanned him in a low, sweeping motion with an oversize straw fan." He said that "the scene was reminiscent of a medieval banquet hall, though the room was not large." He said he and his staff did more listening than talking and that the bishop agreed to support his election. On April 12, the local newspaper, *The Wilmington Journal*, carried a picture of Daddy Grace and a statement he made pledging his support for Dr. Eaton. Daddy Grace stated, in part:

> Our house is a house of prayer for all people. The house of prayer prospers because our people work together . . . If your people did likewise, you might get somewhere.

The candidate surmised that he was impressed by Grace's ability to achieve strength through unity. According to the doctor, Grace's support was valuable to him. He also stated that he "marveled at the showmanship of this man." Unfortunately, Dr. Eaton did not win the election.

3. **Frazier, E. Franklin. *The Negro Church in America*. New York: Schocken Books, 1964, pp. 61-62.**

Dr. Frazier asserts that Daddy Grace's cult was essentially a sect of the holiness type, including conversion, sanctification, and the usual taboos. This cult is distinguished by a physical frenzy in which the sex motive is prominent. With aid of a piano and a drum, the worshippers engage in ecstatic dancing during which, in response to allusions to sex motives, the worshippers cry out, "Daddy, you feel so good." These emotional debauches were generally used to collect money from the members, states the sociologist.

4. **Jones, Charles Edwin. *Black Holiness: A Guide to the Study of Black Participation in Wesleyan Perfectionist and Glossolalic Pentecostal Movements*. Metuchen, NJ: The American Theological Library Association and Scarecrow Press, Inc., 1978, pp. 206-209, 256.**

The compiler surmises that Charles Emmanuel Grace was nineteen years old in 1903, when he arrived in New Bedford, Massachusetts, from the Cape Verde Islands. About 1919, Grace opened the first House of Prayer in a building he himself had built in West Wareham, Massachusetts. In 1927 Grace incorporated the United House of Prayer For All People, Church on the Rock of The Apostolic Faith, in Washington, DC. He concentrated on poverty-scarred urban areas, taking "rocks" that no one else would use to build his church. Grace built churches in New Haven, New York, Buffalo, Philadelphia,

Baltimore, Washington, DC, Newport News, VA, Charlotte, NC, Columbia, SC, Savannah, and Augusta, GA.

5. **Meier, August, and Elliott Rudwick.** *From Plantation to Ghetto.* **New York: Hill and Wang, 1970, pp. 21, 230.**

The authors assert that Daddy Grace and other sect leaders gave their members a sense of self-esteem. Grace's church was called "House of Prayer For All People." The title suggests that everyone was welcome and important. To the poor, his sermons held out the possibility of self-improvement, upward social mobility, and respectability, state the writers. It is said that Sweet Daddy Grace, as he was sometimes called, collected large amounts of money from his followers. The authors contend:

> The dollars which Grace received from the poor who flocked to his services, and which made him a wealthy man, were for the people themselves a small price to pay for the void he filled in their lives.

6. **Nichol, John Thomas.** *Pentecostalism.* **New York: Harper and Row, 1966, pp. 147-151.**

It was argued that for decades the United House of Prayer was a one-man dominated organization led by Sweet Daddy Grace. He founded the church in 1919. Mr. Nichol suggested that Grace was, at one time, a railroad cook-immigrant, cranberry picker. He said Grace owned and administered, among other things, a soap factory, a coffee plantation, an insurance company, and apartment buildings. According to the author, the appeal of Daddy Grace was that "his rites brightened dulled lives, became a focal point of hope for the frustrated and emotionally starved and offered excitement and thrills for everyone." All in all, relatively little is known about Bishop Grace or the United House of Prayer For All People because the group has no literature that can be trusted, states the author.

7. **Peeks, Edward.** *The Long Struggle for Black Power.* **New York: Charles Scribner's Sons, 1971, pp. 243, 253-255.**

Peek recalls that in 1936, during a two-week revival in Savannah, Georgia, Bishop Grace baptized nearly two-thousand converts, each of whom contributed one dollar as part of the baptismal rite. It was brought out that Grace established special low-priced laundries, barber shops, and restaurants in New York and other cities. It was stated: "One way or another, Daddy Grace did become extremely rich, and when he died suddenly on the West coast in 1960, his wealth was variously estimated from $5 million to $25 million. . . ." Grace preached on the subjects of war, peace, and politics. Grace was inclined to be ". . . personal and made reference to those he considered his enemies," concludes the author.

8. **Russell, Ann, and Marjorie Megivern. *North Carolina Portraits of Faith: A Pictorial History of Religions*. Norfolk, VA: The Donning Company, 1986, p. 238.**

    The writers declare that Charles Emmanuel Grace, known as "Sweet Daddy Grace," was revered as the founder of the United House of Prayer For All People, which he started in Charlotte in 1925. The Pentacostal-type denomination spread to many other states and focuses heavily on its charismatic or "Sweet Daddy." The authors assert that in the 1940s and 1950s the Black Bishop C. M. Grace, known as "Daddy Grace," was a popular figure, as was his House of Prayer For All People. Bishop Grace believed in strength through unity, and although he was widely criticized for his flamboyant lifestyle, he exerted great influence in the Black community. Russell and Megivern conclude: "The House of Prayer religious services drew white spectators who watched in awe as "Daddy Grace" exhibited his showmanship."

B. Entries in Encyclopedic Works

9. **Baskin, Wade, and Richard N. Runes.** *Dictionary of Black Culture.* **New York: Philosophical Library, 1973, p. 187.**

   There is a short biographical sketch of Bishop Charles Emmanuel Grace in this collection. He is described as a cult leader and a man of mixed parentage who worked as a cook before he started to preach (1925) and founded the United House of Prayer For All People. It was also stated that erotic dancing was a main feature of the ritual.

10. **Boulware, Marcus H.** *The Oratory of Negro Leaders: 1900-1968.* **Westport, CT: Negro Universities Press, 1969, pp. 208-210.**

    It was surmised that Bishop Charles Emmanuel Grace was sometimes referred to as "the grandiloquent preacher." The writer argues that Daddy Grace built his evangelistic movement on the technique of mixing pageantry, parades, music, uniforms and open-door invitations. The Grace organizations reported 25,000 members in New York City; 25,000 in Newport News, Virginia; 10,000 at Norfolk, Virginia; 120,000 in thirty-one North Carolina cities; and 25,000 in Savannah, Georgia, where the Bishop owned a palatial summer home. The Bishop attracted public attention by employing assembly-line methods in baptisms. Fire department units drenched his converts with water under the blessed administration of Daddy Grace, concludes Professor Boulware.

11. **Bowden, Henry Warner, Editor.** *Dictionary of American Religious Biography.* **Westport, CT: Greenwood Press, 1977, pp. 179-180.**

This short biography discusses Daddy Grace's life. Emphasis was devoted to Grace's religious philosophy. It was stated that the cult leader believed that Grace was the only provision for salvation because all must receive Grace through faith. Bowden also compared Daddy Grace to Father Divine. The author declared that, unlike Father Divine, Grace did not claim divine status.

12. **Clark, Elmer T.** *The Small Sects in America.* **Nashville, TN: Cokesbury Press, 1937, pp. 122-124.**

The author declares that the House of Prayer For All People is one of the most extreme charismatic sects in the country and exhibits features peculiar to itself. It was pointed out that Bishop Grace was not only the creator of the church, but also a dictator of the House of Prayer. Some members of the church did not like the way the church was being run and left the church and started another church (in Augusta, Georgia) and called it "House of Faith." The writer argues that "its devotees are unlettered, emotionally starved, and nervously unstable Negroes drawn from all other sects and from the general population." It was declared that in one city, some citizens considered the House of Prayer a public nuisance or menace to the safety of the community. Daddy Grace adroitly used this situation to create a "martyr psychology," quoting Scripture pertaining to the persecution and suffering of the saints, drawing an exact parallel between the despised early Christians and his hearers, and definitely comparing Bishop Grace to Jesus and Paul, concludes Clark.

13. **Hill, Samuel S., Editor.** *Encyclopedia of Religion in the South.* **Macon, GA: Mercer University Press, 1984, p. 307.**

The editor gives a brief biographical overview of Charles Emmanuel "Sweet Daddy" Grace. Most of this information has appeared in other books. Mr. Hill did point out, however, that "in the early 1920s, Grace told a Winston-Salem, NC, audience that he had raised a sister from the dead." The writer declares that Grace believed that his practices (of healing and baptism) went back to "the faith of the early Christians." The editor concludes that Grace had founded 111 Houses of Prayer For All People and Missions by 1960.

14. **Low, W. Augusta, and Virgil A. Clift, Editors.** *Encyclopedia of Black America.* **New York: McGraw-Hill Book Co., 1981, pp. 668, 823.**

It was stated that Daddy Grace was a very effective evangelist and revivalist between the 1930s and 1950s. He founded the United House of Prayer For All People and was reputed to have amassed a fortune from places of worship and had followers in several American cities, including Savannah, Charlotte, and Washington, DC.

15. **Melton, J. Gordon, Editor.** *The Encyclopedia of American Religions.* **Detroit, MI: Gale Research Co., 1987, pp. 302, 350-351.**

Professor Melton points out that in the 1930s and 1940s, Daddy Grace headed one of the most famous religious groups in the Black community, the United House of Prayer For All People. In doctrine, the church resembles the holiness Pentecostal bodies. It teaches the three experiences: conversion, sanctification, and baptism with the Holy Spirit. The writer concludes that, while the House of Prayer derives from and continues to grow in relation to the Pentecostal framework, the framework was significantly changed by Grace's assumption of deific power. Grace reigned supreme as an autocrat until his death, according to the author.

C. Chapters in Books

16. **Fauset, Arthur Huff.** *Black Gods of the Metropolis: Negro Religious Cults in the Urban North.* **Philadelphia: University of Pennsylvania Press, 1944, pp. 22-30, 69, 70, 73-75, 77-78, 85, 89, 111-113.**

    Chapter III is entitled, "United House of Prayer For All People." This chapter discusses the "Origin," "Organization," "Membership," "Finance," "Sacred Text," "Beliefs," "Ritual," and "Practices" of the United House of Prayer For All People. The author attended several of the church services of this cult and gives examples of typical services. It was also pointed out that Bishop Grace had been heard admonishing his followers:

    > Never mind about God. Salvation is by Grace only . . . . Grace has given God a vacation, and since God is on His vacation, don't worry Him . . . . If you sin against God, Grace can save you, but if you sin against Grace, God cannot save you.

    Scriptural references by the dozens, in which the word "grace" appears, are quoted to demonstrate that "this man Grace" is the spirit of God walking among men, concludes the writer.

17. **Georgia Writers' Project.** *Drums and Shadows: Survival Studies Among Georgia Coastal Negroes.* **Athens: University of Georgia Press, 1940, pp. 46-51.**

There is a chapter in this book that discusses Daddy Grace's visit to Brownville, a Black community along the edge of Savannah, Georgia. The writer visited the House of Prayer and gives a detailed description of what went on. He observed that many members of the church testified to the miracles that Bishop Grace had performed on their behalf. During the services, Daddy Grace spoke. The theme of his address was, "Whatsoever a man soweth, that also shall he reap." The main issue, however, was often sidetracked, and the speaker commented upon world politics, the war (World War II), anecdotes of his trips abroad, his persecution by enemies, all of whom "the Lord struck down dead," and the general condition of the local community, states the writer. Daddy Grace advised his followers strongly against trusting anyone. "If the angel from Heaven comes down and wants an extra pair of wings, don't trust him," he warned. "Tell him you ain't got no time to keep books today. He has to pay cash." Toward the end of his talk, the Bishop said he could accomplish anything he chose, even sinking ships, destroying fleets of planes, or conquering entire nations. He was not the actual power, he said, but he was so close to it that he had only to reach out his hand and pull the switch, concludes the author.

18. **Hall, Gordon Langley. *The Sawdust Trail: The Story of American Evangelism*. Philadelphia: Macrae Smith Co., 1964, pp. 163-170.**

Chapter Seven is entitled "Prophet in a Long Fur Coat: 'Daddy' Grace, 1883-1960." Most of the information on Daddy Grace in this chapter is well known. The author does mention a number of things that are not too well known, such as, according to Hall, Grace spoke six languages, including Hebrew. Much of the data in the essay is based on Daddy Grace and his relationship with his House of Prayer For All People in Augusta, Georgia. Hall concluded:

'Sweet Daddy' had the last laugh on his critics. He had willed back (after his death) to his church most of those green dollar bills (estimated to be $25 million) he had so often been accused of hoarding.

19. **Mathison, Richard R. *Faiths, Cults, and Sects in America. From Atheism to Zen*. Indianapolis, IN: Bobbs-Merrill, 1960, pp. 240-258.**

Chapter 34 is devoted to "Sweet Daddy Grace." The author observes that Grace was said to have owned a soap factory, a coffee plantation, an insurance company, the tallest apartment building in the world, hotels, fabulous mansions and castles. It was said that he was dubbed the "boyfriend of the world." The writer suggests that Sweet Daddy doctrine was simple: A true believer could meet with the Holy Spirit through "gifts." In practice, his rites brightened dulled lives, became a focal point of hope for the frustrated and emotionally starved and offered excitement and thrills for everyone, concludes Mathison.

D. Daddy Grace Compared to Other
Black Religious Leaders

20. **Baer, Hans A. *The Black Spiritual Movement: A Religious Response to Racism*. Knoxville: University of Tennessee Press, 1984, pp. 143-145.**

   Daddy Grace is compared to Father Divine, Father Hurley, and other Black cult leaders. Dr. Baer states that Daddy Grace was a Black God and flamboyant but less famous than Father Divine. It was observed that Daddy Grace was thought of as a God by many of his followers. Some of his converts saw him as the Savior and the Spirit of Jesus Incarnated. Even during Grace's lifetime, his followers said prayers, knelt, and genuflected before the picture of their Savior (Daddy Grace), concluded the author.

21. **Burnham, Kenneth E. *God Comes to America: Father Divine and the Peace Mission Movement*. Boston: Lambeth Press, 1979, pp. 29, 155.**

   Daddy Grace was seen as a self-styled emissary of God by Father Divine. He had little respect for Daddy Grace and other self-styled emissaries of God who wore robes and elaborate garb he considered fit only for pastors, preachers and ministers. Father Divine said God does not need them. He never appeared in clerical clothing. Divine once declared, referring to Daddy Grace and others, "I could try to make myself look pretty, too, but I forbid!"

22. **Clark, Kenneth B.** *Dark Ghetto: Dilemmas of Social Power.* **New York: Harper and Row, 1965, pp. 174-175.**

Dr. Clark discusses the power of the church. He contends that established Black churches, the many storefront churches, and sporadic Black quasireligious cult groups, like Daddy Grace and Father Divine's followers, play chiefly a cathartic role for Blacks. He concludes, in part: "The churches and cults and their leaders provide an opportunity for their followers to 'let off steam,' to seek release for emotions which cannot be expressed in overcrowded homes or on the job. . . ."

23. **Harris, Sara.** *Father Divine.* **New York: Collier Books, 1971, pp. xi, 50-56.**

It was pointed out that of all the flourishing Harlem cult leaders of 1933, the most successful was a man called Daddy Grace. The writer states that Daddy Grace was much more popular in the South than Father Divine. In fact, Grace continued to fight against Father Divine. Daddy Grace once purchased a building in Harlem, New York, that housed Father Divine's main headquarters and put him and his followers out of the building. After Divine left the headquarters, Grace started to operate there in an attempt to take over Divine followers. Daddy Grace was unsuccessful in keeping Divine's members. Father Divine opened another headquarters in Harlem and his followers went with him.

24. **Essien-Udom, E. U.** *Black Nationalism: A Search for an Identity in America.* **New York: Dell Publishing Co., 1964, p. 213.**

Dr. Essien-Udom states that the Nation of Islam and its leaders compare Daddy Grace to other religious cults and saw all of them little more than a joke. It was argued, in part: "We [Negro Americans] must wake up and see that such leaders as Father Divine, Daddy Grace (deceased), Prophet Jones and the likes are a big joke and cannot get the so-called Negro anything but ridiculous before the eyes of the civilized world."

25. **Jones, Raymond Julius.** *A Comparative Study of Religious Cult Behavior Among Negroes with Special References to Emotional Group Conditioning Factors.* **Washington, DC: Graduate School of Howard University, 1939, pp. 304, 9, 15, 125.**

It was pointed out that the United House of Prayer For All People's entire program seemed designed so as to emphasize and magnify the personality of Bishop Charles Emanuel "Daddy" Grace, the leader of the cult. Bishop Grace is represented as being the "human repository of the grace and bounty of God." Dr. Jones stated that this and other cults are reminiscent of the periodic outburst of "messianic" religious fervor that had marked the pages of religious history for many centuries. The author asserted that Daddy Grace and other cult leaders came into conflicts with the civil authorities on several occasions, one of the most recent of which terminated in the closing of one of his House of Prayer For All People churches in the state of North Carolina. Grace was also compared to Father Divine as a platform speaker. It was concluded that he (Father Divine) did not "have any of the gaudiness of the preposterous 'Daddy Grace'. . . ."

26. **Ottley, Roi. *New World A-Coming*. Boston: Houghton Mifflin Co., 1943, pp. 93-95.**

Professor Ottley contends that Father Divine had sharp competition from Daddy Grace for his followers. The writer declares that Grace began hijacking Divine's followers by vigorous spiritual enticements. The author surmises that, in the course of several years, Grace amassed a fortune from what some Negroes called 'the Jesus racket.' His frequent clashes with the law over matters of an extreme worldly nature served only to increase the attendance and the collections, and also to give the Bishop much desired publicity, concludes the author. Mr. Ottley also writes that "Bishop Grace's movement never made much impression on Harlem (New York)—Daddy Grace only took but never gave!"

27. **Rodney, Carlisle. *The Roots of Black Nationalism*. Port Washington, NY: Kennikat Press, 1975, pp. 137-139.**

The writer declares that while not claiming to be God, the head of the United House of Prayer believed that salvation was "by Grace alone." It was stated that Bishop Grace attacked Father Divine as a charlatan, and Divine cursed him. Rodney concludes that cult leaders such as Grace and Divine did not appeal to Black nationalists and Black intellectuals.

28. **Vincent, Theodore G. *Black Power and the Garvey Movement*. Berkeley, CA: Ramparts Press, 1971, pp. 208, 222.**

The writer surmises that "former Garveyites see in Father Divine, evangelist George Wilson, Bishop Grace and others the incarnation of Marcus Garvey." It was also suggested that Grace and Divine and other such movements are a form of escape to other worldly movements.

29. **Washington, Joseph R. *Black Sects and Cults*. Garden City, NY: Doubleday, 1972, pp. 10-11, 15-16, 77, 127, 149, 158-159.**

The author compares Daddy Grace to Father Divine, Prophet Cherry and Elijah Muhammad. He states that Daddy Grace's cult was a business enterprise for him. All church offerings go directly to him and his strict control of all money cannot be questioned. The writer asserts that Daddy Grace's appeal was through Holiness and Pentecostal emotionalism to women who worshipped him. Dr. Washington concludes:

> At his death in 1960, his estate was estimated to be in the millions. Essentially, this movement was a profit-making business venture by a black entrepreneur who succeeded by manipulating spiritual hunger into a system of self-aggrandizement.

30. **Weisbrot, Robert. *Father Divine and the Struggle for Racial Equality*. Urbana, IL: University of Illinois Press, 1983, pp. 41-42, 191, 229.**

The writer suggests that whatever the intangible joys Daddy Grace afforded his followers, he evinced no clear program to treat the deeper social and economic problems that corroded his followers' lives. Grace's gestures at philanthropy often had only symbolic value, such as the free banquet at the end of his annual convocations, states Dr. Weisbrot. Such largesses as Daddy Grace bestowed was, in any case, little more than a fig leaf for the relentless assaults he conduced on his followers' meager wealth, according to the author. Professor Weisbrot concludes, in part: "Rather, his [Daddy Grace] success as an evangelical predator despite his transparent greed, remains an enduring tribute to human credulity. . . ."

31. **Wilson, Jeremiah Moses. *Black Messiahs and Uncle Toms: Social Literary Manipulations of a Religious Myth*. University Park, PA: Pennsylvania State University Press, 1982, pp. 11-12, 125, 163.**

The writer contends that of all of the cult leaders, Bishop Grace was clearly the most opportunistic of them. His doctrine consisted of little more than a play on words. Since salvation was by grace alone, "Grace" was more important to salvation than was God, declares the author. It was stated that the cult leader had no social program and that he sought to deify himself, rather than to stir up the political passion of Black people. Professor Wilson concludes that Bishop Grace, like the other "Black gods of the metropolis"—Prophet Cherry and Father Divine—was flamboyant and egotistical. They used the method of mass hypnotism, argues the writer.

II

THESES, DISSERTATIONS AND UNPUBLISHED MANUSCRIPTS

A Selected List

32. **Eddy, G. Norman.** *The True Believers: Some Impressions of American Deviant Religions.* **Unpublished Manuscript, Boston University College of General Education, 1962, pp. 36-45.**

Professor Eddy declares that Bishop Grace allowed his disciples to believe that he is eternal and that he was present at the crucifixion of Christ. . . . Regardless of what he believed about himself, his followers looked upon him with worshipful regard. In every sanctuary, they have pictures of him in the flowing robes and the sacred bleeding heart associated with Christ, concludes Dr. Eddy.

33. **Tyms, James Daniel.** *A Study of Fourth Religious Cults Operating Among Negroes.* **Unpublished Thesis, Howard University, 1938, pp. 52-78.**

Chapter II is devoted to Bishop Charles M. Grace and The House of Prayer For All People. The author suggests that Grace started his first mission in Houston, Texas, in 1921. It appears that the cult leaders started out holding church services in large tents in Charlotte, North Carolina, and in Newport News, Virginia, in the mid-1920s. Mr. Tyms compares Bishop Grace with Father Divine, Elder Solomon Lightfoot Michaux, Bishop Taylor, and other cult leaders. He also discusses the various legal problems Grace was involved in: embezzlement, the Mann

Act, tax evasion, and damages by one of his members. In the 1930s his movement had churches in seven states: North Carolina, South Carolina, New York, Virginia, Maryland, Georgia, and Pennsylvania. There was also a church in the District of Columbia. There were two divisions of the House of Prayer, the missions and the churches. There is also *The Grace Magazine*, the monthly publication of the activities of the House of Prayer For All People. The objectives of the magazine were:

1. To unfold the hidden truth of the Gospel.

2. To magnify the life of Christ.

3. To teach to appreciate the gift of God.

4. To testify of the thousands and healing of the millions.

In addition to the above objectives of the magazine, there were four other objectives of the House of Prayer For All People. They were:

1. To save souls through preaching repentance.

2. It aims at establishing the House of Prayer throughout the land. It is the way by which man is to be saved.

3. To wrought changes in individual lives by helping them to get the Holy Ghost.

4. To create a consciousness of sanctification and holiness which are needed if men are to inherit the Kingdom.

The author includes a number of testimonies in this thesis. All of the testimonies praised Sweet Daddy Grace for his healing power upon them.

34. **Whiting, Albert N. *The United House of Prayer For All People: A Case Study of a Charismatic Sect.* Unpublished Doctoral Dissertation, American University, 1952, 319 pp.**

This is the only doctoral dissertation that I found that dealt with the House of Prayer and its founder, Daddy Grace. Dr. Whiting visited many of the churches in Washington, DC, and interviewed several members of that body. The writer compares this sect with other sects in the United States. Chapter III discusses "Origin and Distribution," "Organization," "Beliefs," "Practices and Ritual," and "Summary," of the

United House of Prayer. Chapter IV deals with "Sex," "Age," "Marital Status," "Education," "Income," "Housing," "Previous Religious Affiliations," "Reasons for Joining the House of Prayer," and "Summary," of the United House of Prayer. Chapter V analyzes the lives of ten members of the United House of Prayer. Nearly one-third of this dissertation (85 pages) was devoted to those case studies. In the writer's Summary and Conclusions, he discusses "The Sectarian Characteristics of the House of Prayer." Appendix A deals with "Composite Study for Rorschach Data Gathered on 19 Cases of Persons Belonging to the Daddy Grace Sect." There are "Personality Summaries For Each Rorschach Record" of the 19 cases. A 5-page Bibliography rounds out this work. Various references are made to Daddy Grace throughout this study. Dr. Whiting concludes, in part:

> . . . The people attracted to the House of Prayer came out of situations characterized by unsatisfying interpersonal relations and various psychological problems related to frustration and rejection, particularly in the early years of life, illnesses of a psychosomatic variety and emotional insecurity. . . .

It was also surmised that The House of Prayer served as a refuge for the economically deprived, culturally marginal, emotionally disturbed, and introversively inclined. The church did give its followers a rather deep sense of individual worth and "belongingness . . . ." Finally, and in relation to the purely religious aspects of the sect, an undeniable concreteness is given to the meaning of life in the knowledge of the fact that God is near and real, through the medium of Grace, and that under his guidance, they (the followers) are destined for the promises of the elect in the eternal life, according to Dr. Whiting.

35. **Williams, Chancellor.** *The Socio-Economic Significance of the Store-Front Church Movement in the United States Since 1920.* **Unpublished Doctoral Dissertation, American University, 1949, pp. 116-144.**

Chapter 5 discusses Daddy Grace. It was pointed out that the limited intelligence of the great masses of people was the chief basis of the powerful organization which Daddy Grace built. Dr. Williams visited several House of Prayer churches in Baltimore, Philadelphia and Washington, DC, over a four-year period and observed, first hand, Daddy Grace and his followers. The historian declares that the House of Prayer had a number of white members. Bishop Grace spent practically all of his time making tours of his churches. Prof. Williams asserts that Grace's tour of his churches was one great and endless fund-raising activity. His income ran into the millions of dollars, states the author. Dr. Williams argues:

> Grace's attitude toward his followers actually seems to be one
> of haughty contempt. . . .   The man himself is not at all
> interested in the welfare of his followers. . . .   They are
> exploited. Religion is his business . . . .

The author concludes, in part:

> Charles M. Grace does not claim to be God, but forthwith places
> himself on equal ground with the Almighty and actually replaces
> Jesus Christ by taking possession of "all the keys to Heaven."

III
ARTICLES

A. Major Articles

36. **"America's Richest Negro Minister: Daddy Grace Heads Religious Empire Worth $10 Million, Claims He Is Neither Wealthy nor Negro,"** *Ebony*, Vol. 8, No. 2, January 1952, pp. 17-23.

    The author states that Daddy Grace was one of America's most successful evangelists who built a vast religious movement on frenzy, pageantry and endless monetary contributions. This article asserts that Grace said he was neither a colored man nor wealthy. He said: "I am not a colored man. I am from the white race. I was born in Portugal." It was observed that at another time the Bishop was heard saying, "I am a colorless bishop. Sometimes I am black, sometimes I am white. I preach to all races." Finance was the bedrock of Daddy Grace's church and the rituals made it plain that raising money was the most important item on a prayer meeting's agenda. The cult as a whole placed a powerful emphasis upon money and means of persuading the brethren to make contributions. Giving to Daddy Grace was a spiritual obligation of the church from which followers derived a strange, sometimes ecstatic delight, concludes the article.

37. **"Bishop Buys Tallest Apartment Building; Daddy Does It Again!,"** *Pittsburgh Courier*, May 16, 1958, pp. 1, 4.

    Daddy Grace purchased the fabulous "El Dorado" at 300 Center Park West, New York City, which was reported to be the tallest apartment house building in the world. Grace stated that the income from the property would be used for the "betterment and welfare" of the members of his church. The building had 216 apartments, 1,310 rooms and 675 bathrooms. Many of the apartments had private terrace and most had wood-burning fireplaces. The building contained thirteen elevators.

38. **"Bishop 'Daddy' Grace Challenges Harlem Cleric and Other Critics,"** *Chicago Defender*, **September 6, 1947, p. 2**

Daddy Grace challenged his critics to "prove my (his) doctrine false." He offered $1,000,000 to anyone who would get on the radio and convince his followers otherwise and predicted that the new South would become a reality when regardless of race and color, the people learn to stand together. Grace had recently purchased $2,000,000 worth of Harlem (New York) property. He assured his followers that he intended to set the pace for leaders of the church. The Bishop argued:

> Am I going to do that . . . by demonstrating beyond any reasonable doubt that spiritual and economic power is the world's most formidable weapon for peace and happiness?

He also declared, in part:

> Instead of filling my own pocket . . . I have invested money entrusted to me in valuable real estate holdings. This property belongs to the members of the House of Prayer. . . .

39. **"Bishop Daddy Grace Has Big Convention,"** *Pittsburgh Courier*, **October 10, 1936, p. 7.**

About 2,500 followers of Daddy Grace attended the 10th Annual House of Prayer Convention in Columbia, South Carolina. Grace said he was on a tour of many cities: Philadelphia, Pennsylvania; Washington, DC; Newport News, VA; Charlotte, NC; Savannah, Georgia; and Augusta, Georgia. The convention ended with a big parade and public baptizing.

40. **"Bishop 'Daddy' Grace Honored in Charlotte as Hundreds of Followers Stage Big Parade,"** *Winston-Salem Journal*, **September 8, 1947, p. 15.**

It was estimated that 25,000 persons stood under a boiling sun in Charlotte, North Carolina, for two hours to see a religious parade led by Bishop C. M. Grace. It was stated that it was "one of the largest" ever held in Charlotte. The event climaxed the Twenty-first Annual Grace Holy Convocation Week and was preceded by a baptizing for 350 convert at the House of Prayer's pool. There also were converts of Daddy Grace from other North Carolina cities: Wilmington, Rocky Mount, Statesville, Dallas, and Durham, as well as followers from Lancaster, South Carolina, and many other places.

41. **"Bishop Grace Robbed of $4,000 Cash,"** *Philadelphia Tribune,* **September 28, 1939, p. 1.**

Bishop Grace was robbed of $4,000 in Savannah, Georgia, while he was asleep. Bishop Grace reported the theft to police on Monday morning and stated that the money was in $100 and $50 bills. Bishop Grace had conducted a big celebration in the city on the night the reported theft took place. Three persons held for investigation were later released.

42. **"Bishop Grace's Followers Will Stage Parade, Baptismal Rites,"** *Charlotte News,* **September 11, 1938, p. 10.**

This article stated that Bishop Grace came to Charlotte, North Carolina, about 12 years ago (ca. 1926) and established this as one of the first of a line of churches which extended over the greater part of the length of the Atlantic seaboard of the United States. It was pointed out that the Bishop was early recognized among Negroes, in Charlotte, as being the "Black Christ," possessing celestial powers of exceeding potency.

43. **Butler, George. "25,000 Persons Defy Hot Sun to See Daddy Grace's Parade,"** *Charlotte Observer,* **September 8, 1947, p. B-1.**

It was estimated that more than 25,000 persons stood under a boiling sun for two hours in Charlotte to see a religious parade led by Bishop C. M. Grace. The local police said it was one of the largest ever held in Charlotte. Virtually everyone in the parade wore a uniform. Grace rode at the end of the parade in a jeep, painted red, white, and blue, and bearing many of his messages. The leader addressed his followers over a portable amplifying system during the parade. At the conclusion of the parade, Bishop Grace addressed his followers and said religion and fun should not be separated and urged plenty of "beefsteak and fried chicken" for his followers. The event climaxed the twenty-first annual Grace Holy Convocation week and was preceded by a baptism for 380 converts at the House of Prayer pool, asserted Butler.

44. **Casey, Phil. "Daddy Grace Came a Long Way from Early Days in New Bedford,"** *Washington Post*, **March 7, 1960, p. B-1.**

The reporter states that Daddy Grace usually traveled on the road about 300 days a year, baptizing thousands in river and under fire hoses, catching attention everywhere with his long, red, white and blue fingernails, his shoulder-length hair and his colorful cutaway and flashy jewelry. It was stated that, at one time, Daddy Grace allegedly raised his sister from the dead. Grace was quoted as saying:

> All of our meetings are conducted under the directions of the Holy Ghost. If we are directed to sing, we sing; and if we are called upon to exhort, we exhort. . . . We also have the power to heal, and the most devoted members of our congregations are those who have been healed.

45. _____. **"Daddy's Money Grew on Trees (Man-Made),"** *Washington Post*, **March 11, 1960, pp. B-1, B-12.**

It was stated that Daddy Grace's House of Prayer did not have three million followers, but only about 100,000. If the movement had but 50,000 members turning in 50 cents a week, it still would have had a revenue of about $1.3 million. Grace's biggest following was in Charlotte, North Carolina, where about 12,000 people are reported to be members of Grace's United House of Prayer For All People, surmised the reporter.

46. _____. **"Daddy's Outstanding Miracle: Hold on Flock,"** *Washington Post*, **March 13, 1960, p. B-5.**

According to this writer, the followers of Daddy Grace were not supposed to swear, smoke, drink, dance or go to the movies. Daddy Grace was against all these things, plus war, airplanes and adultery. It was stated that one effect of Daddy Grace's movement was that it reduced crime. Frank Littlejohn, a retired Charlotte, North Carolina, police officer surmised: "It was the rarest thing in the world to see any of his members in any criminal trouble. He was really an asset." Daddy Grace's physician had this to say about the cult leader:

> He did more good than harm. In a battlefield, he grew some flowers. He was a pretty good Joe. He should make purgatory, and that about as well as most of us will do.

47. _____. **"Friends Say Daddy Didn't Need Money; He Had Everything,"** *Washington Post*, **March 10, 1960, p. A-26.**

Mr. Casey interviewed Samuel H. Keets, a long-time friend of Daddy Grace. Mr. Keets declared that if you could get Grace to commit himself "his word was 100 per cent." Keets says Grace established the Family Aid Association for the House of Prayer. Followers paid a membership fee and small monthly dues; and Daddy got 25 per cent off the top. Grace lost interest in the association and it became defunct. The Rev. E. Franklin Jackson, president of the Washington, DC, chapter of the NAACP, stated that there was no record that Daddy Grace was ever any help to that organization. Rev. Jackson concluded that Grace "didn't develop civic responsibility in his followers."

48. _____. **"Grace Attorneys Sue to Free Million in Cash,"** *Washington Post*, **May 10, 1960, p. B-1.**

Jules H. Sigal, tax consultant to the United House of Prayer For All People, said that Bishop Grace held close to $900,000 in his name as trustee for the church and in the church's name in the American Security and Trust Company. The consultant, an attorney, was seeking the money on behalf of the House of Prayer. The Internal Revenue Service had liens on Daddy Grace's estate totaling $5.9 million. The Government claimed he owed them that amount in back taxes. His attorneys argued that Grace held the money in his name as a trustee of the church and, therefore, not taxable. Casey pointed out that Sweet Daddy Grace held more than $3 million in cash as trustee of the church or in the church's name in more than 75 bank accounts in about 50 towns and cities. In some instances, the money was listed simply under his name, according to the reporter.

49. _____. **"Many Setbacks Failed to Deter Daddy Grace,"** *Washington Post*, **March 8, 1960, pp. B-1, B-4.**

Mr. Casey asserted that Daddy Grace brought Father Divine's "Heaven" missions in Harlem, New York, but Grace did not want to drive him out of Harlem. Grace was reported to have declared about Divine:

> I will not drive him out of Harlem. I will just let him stay. Poor fellow. Let him stay. I will give him peace and pity. I'm a servant of man. Let him stay.

Father Divine, nevertheless left Harlem and set up quarters elsewhere, declaring he had willed it anyway. It was also stated in this article that

Daddy Grace married a Mexican woman for his second wife and that he had a son by her. Grace left $10,000 in his will to this son, according to the reporter. Despite the worship of Daddy Grace as a person, there is no evidence he ever claimed to be God, although many of his followers worshipped him as a God, observed Casey.

50. _____. **"Parables Served Daddy to Evade Direct Replies,"** *Washington Post,* **March 9, 1960, pp. B-1, B-12.**

The reporter stated that Daddy Grace generally would not answer questions directly. Instead, he would use parables to evade direct response. To Grace, everybody was "honey." When asked about his home, he replied, "Purity, isn't it, honey?" The House of Prayer that he founded had many members, he'd say, "Millions, honey. They love me." "Love of money is not the root of all evil," he might say, and then, "Never let your left hand know what the right hand is doing." Mr. Casey interviewed some of Grace's converts and concluded, disappointedly:

> There seems no clue as to how the former short-order cook, patent medicine and sewing machine salesman and grocer suddenly, in his middle years, became a religious symbol to hundreds of thousands of Negroes on the East and West Coast.

51. _____. **"U. S. Settles Bishop Grace's Tax Bill for $1,940,000; District Is Next,"** *Washington Post,* **June 3, 1961, p. B-1.**

Mr. Casey stated that after 15 years, the Internal Revenue Service finally caught up with the late Charles M. Grace and collected nearly $2 million from his estate. The Government originally wanted $5.9 million for taxes that he allegedly owed them. A settlement was made between the government and the United House of Prayer For All People for nearly $2 million. Both the government and the House of Prayer gained something from the settlement. The Government assessed the estate only $967,581 and nearly $1 million in interest and penalties. The United House of Prayer For All People was recognized as a church, with its income not subject to taxes. The House of Prayer was also trying to come to some settlement with the Washington, DC, Government, which was seeking $78,853 in estate taxes. Bishop Grace had a home and headquarters in Washington, DC, as well as other property holdings in that city.

52. **"City Buys Grace Site for School,"** *Standard Times* **(New Bedford, MA), March 26, 1962, pp. 1, 9.**

The city of New Bedford purchased C. M. Grace Property on County Street for $31,731. The city planned to put a new school on part of the property. The property included 49,481 square feet. It took more than two years to complete the transactions because of the various suits against Grace's estate. The city withheld $9,124 for back taxes owed by the estate of Grace.

53. **Clayton, James. "Bishop Grace Support Suit Jams Court,"** *Washington Post,* **December 20, 1957, p. A-3.**

Mrs. Louvenia A. Royster sued Daddy Grace for alimony, claiming that they were married in 1923. Bishop Grace denied such a marriage ever took place. More than 100 of Grace's followers jammed the courtroom of District Court in Washington, DC, and steadfastly clung to their seats. Daddy Grace attended the trial and wore a brown tailored cutaway with a flashy red tie and a large gold tie clasp, declared Clayton. The reporter stated that Grace was 74 years old and came to the United States from Portugal in 1900 and founded the United House of Prayer For All People in 1919. Attorney Franklin Yasmer represented the bishop at the trial.

54. _____. **"Court Curbs Grace Holy Land Lecture,"** *Washington Star,* **January 10, 1958, p. B-1.**

The reporter commented on Daddy Grace's court appearance while he was on trial in Washington, DC, for allegedly having married Mrs. Louvenia A. Royster. Bishop Grace argued that he could not have possibly married Mrs. Royster because, at the time that she said he married her, he was in the Near East visiting the Holy Land. According to Grace on Christmas night, in 1923, he "spent all night in the manger." The next day, he declared, that he went out to the shepherds' fields where the angels sang, "Glory to God in the Highest, Peace on Earth. Good will toward men." Daddy Grace also described one picture among his souvenirs as showing him "kneeling down in the Egyptian sand where Moses, a Hebrew boy, became the Pharaoh's favorite." Undergoing cross examination later in the day, the evangelist said he was once ordained to preach in San Francisco but he could not recall who ordained him or precisely where it was. He was also asked the name of the organization that performed the ceremony. Grace, answered, "an evangelistic Faith or something like that." The trial had been going on for ten days. There was also a picture of Daddy Grace dressed in a purple jacket with black velvet and gold trim and a black and chartreuse vest. The photo was made in his home at 11 Logan

Circle in Washington, DC. There was also a bust of Grace in the photo, in front of a large cross.

55. _____. **"Daddy Grace ordered to Halt Court Collections,"** *Washington Star***, January 3, 1958, p. B-4.**

During Bishop Grace's trial for alleged abandonment, the leader's followers kept giving money to him. Judge Alexander Holtzoff told Grace that it is objectionable and a violation of the rules prohibiting solicitation of money in government buildings and that he would not permit it. He also told Grace that if he did not stop he would have him arrested for disorderly conduct. When Grace's attorney, Franklin Yasmer, said that the Bishop does not ask for money, the judge replied, "Well, he can refuse. He can walk away from them." The trouble, according to the court officials, was the evangelist's habit of accepting money and passing out candy to his followers. The trial concerned Mrs. Louvenia A. Royster's contentions that Bishop Grace married her under the name of Royster in 1923 in New York, and she was now seeking support.

56. _____. **"Judge Sees Bad Grace Calling Bishop Daddy,"** *Washington Post***, December 21, 1957, p. A-3.**

In the trial against Daddy Grace by Mrs. Louvenia A. Royster for alimony, Judge Alexander Holtzoff stopped Attorney Jesse H. Chessin the first time Chessin referred to the leader as "Daddy Grace." The judge declared, in part: "Call him Grace, call him Royster, but don't call him Daddy. . . . Please don't call people by their nicknames in this court." The judge also declared that he had never heard of Daddy Grace until the trial began. Bishop Grace denied having married Mrs. Royster in 1923.

57. _____. **"Share of Daddy Grace's Treasure in Back Taxes Sought by Uncle Sam,"** *Washington Post***, February 2, 1960, p. B-1.**

Mr. Clayton stated that the Internal Revenue Service claimed that Daddy Grace owed nearly $6 millon dollars in back income taxes. The tax collectors stated that Grace neglected to pay taxes on his personal income between 1945 and 1957. The income that the leader received in those years came largely from his three million followers. The nickels and dimes they contributed and the investments the nickels and dimes bought left the holdings of the House of Prayer For All People and Daddy Grace about $25 million when he died, according to the writer.

It was also pointed out that the tax collectors had filed liens and levies only on assets held in one of Daddy Grace's four names. They were filed in Washington, DC, Maryland, Virginia, Pennsylvania, Georgia, North Carolina, South Carolina, Connecticut, New York, Massachusetts, Ohio, New Jersey, Florida, and Michigan.

58. _____. "U. S. Sues 'Daddy Grace's Estate' for Evasion of $5.9 Million in Taxes," *Washington Star*, February 2, 1990, p. 1.

The reporter declared that the Internal Revenue Service said Daddy Grace failed to pay about $5,990,000 in back income taxes over a twelve-year period prior to 1957. The income which the leader received in those years came largely from his three million followers, who contributed their nickels and dimes.

59. "Court Closes Daddy Grace's Dixie Church," *New York Amsterdam News*, October 29, 1938, p. 1.

It was asserted that the South Carolina State Supreme Court declared that the City of Columbia was warranted in calling the House of Prayer a public nuisance and ordered it closed. The court action was the result of a petition signed by 232 residents of the House of Prayer neighborhoods complaining about the noise made during the church service. The court ruled that:

> . . . the evidence showed that there is dancing carried on in the church, weird noises and music, shouting, stamping of the feet, unearthly sounds, use of drums, trombones, horns and scrubbing boards and that the services would be heard from early hours of the evening until the early hours of the morning, night after night, day after day.

60. Crawford, Marc. "Daddy's Multi-Colored Castle Has Rich Neighbors Seeing Red," *Jet*, March 23, 1957, pp. 46-49.

Daddy Grace purchased Prophet Jones' 54-room house in Detroit and immediately had it painted red, white and blue. His neighbors were outraged and felt he made their neighborhood a laughing stock, lowered property values and disgraced Detroit society. Grace stated, "A man's got a right to paint his house any color he wants to. And my house, the Bible says, shall be called the house of prayer." He continued to surmise: "But . . . I want everybody to know I am a good Daddy and I love all of my children on Arden Park. If they are hungry, I'll feed them."

61. **Cullinane, Kevin. "'Yes, Sweet Daddy,'"** *Washington (DC) Daily News*, **January 16, 1958, p. 18.**

   The reporter visited Daddy Grace at one of the services of the United House of Prayer For All People in Washington, DC. Bishop Grace talked about his trial and how a woman was suing him for desertion. She also claimed that she was married to the evangelist. The leader declared:

   > Now you see why everyone wants to say they are my wife. They see this money. . . . But you know I never been married in my life. I'm happy to be with you and I'm glad to see you all so happy. Are you happy?

   He continued: "Love of money is the root of all evil. . . . They're (the congregation) all my children. . . . I love them all." Mr. Cullinane observed that mothers tucked dollar bills into their babies' clothes and brought them forward to Daddy Grace's white throne.

62. **"Daddy Grace Buys $1 Million Mansion,"** *Pittsburgh Courier*, **March 15, 1958, p. 1.**

   Daddy Grace bought a $1,000,000, Berkeley Square mansion in Los Angeles for a reported $450,000 in cash. It was stated that this one made 41 houses that he owned. This mansion had 85 rooms and was immediately repainted red, white, and blue. This article declared that Daddy Grace told the reporters that "the Lord had sent" him to America to help the people here. He concluded: "God was never in America until I brought him here."

63. **"Daddy Grace Denies Dixie Birth, Says He's 'Portuguese Subject' in Alimony Suit,"** *Jet*, **January 23, 1958, pp. 18-19.**

   This article stated that Daddy denied that he was ever married to Mrs. Louvenia A. Royster who claimed she was married to him. The leader said the day that she supposedly married him, he was on a ship going to the Holy Land. He said he was not a citizen of the United States, but was a "subject of Portugal." America's richest cultist said: "I do not know this woman. All she wants is my money."

64. **"Daddy Grace Encircled by 'Angels,' 'Cherubs,' as He Rides Three Cities' Streets,"** *Norfolk Journal and Guide*, **July 11, 1936, pp. 1, 10.**

Daddy Grace visited Norfolk, Virginia, and rode on one of the floats in the Fourth of July parade. According to this article, Grace created quite a sensation in the local House of Prayer when he demanded that his constituents present him $1,000 before he left Norfolk. He stipulated that $500 was to be in silver. It was not disclosed if the church gave him the $1,000. One of the many themes discussed by the visiting cult leader was sexual perversion among women. He is reported to have said: "I will shine my shoes on any woman I catch in the act of another man."

65. **"Daddy Grace Left Legacy of $10 Million and Litigation,"** *Washington Post*, **June 12, 1960, p. B-2.**

According to this writer, Daddy Grace, in his imperturbable and inscrutable way, left a legacy that condemned everyone concerned to more days in court than they could bear. The federal government (IRS), the city of Washington (DC), a number of states, members of the House of Prayer For All People, and several government and private attorneys were all bewildered by the litigations. The main question centered on whether Daddy Grace's United House of Prayer For All People of the Church on the Rock of the Apostolic Faith was a church or a business. Daddy Grace constantly maintained when he was alive that he had no personal money and that everything belonged to the United House of Prayer. He left all but $70,500 to the church. At one time, more than 36 attorneys were involved in the litigations. One lawyer observed: "When they (attorneys) get together, it's a convention."

66. **"Daddy Grace, Millionaire With a Bible,"** *Our World*, **Vol. 8, October 1953, pp. 50-53.**

The writer claimed that Grace was a very wealthy man. The cult leader stated that he was not. Daddy Grace declared that he had no money of his own and his church supplied all of his financial needs.

67. **"Daddy Grace Pays $450,000 for Los Angeles, Calif., Mansion,"** *Jet*, **March 20, 1958, p. 20.**

Daddy Grace bought a $1,000,000, 85-room mansion in the swank Berkeley Square section of Los Angeles as a West Coast haven for his followers. The showplace had a swimming pool, a grand ballroom with a $17,000 piano and $230,000 in Oriental rugs, Ming vases and artwork. He had it painted red, white and blue.

68. **"Daddy Grace Plans $6 Million Resort near New Haven, Conn.,"** *Afro-American*, **September 5, 1959, p. 6.**

This article states that Daddy Grace planned to purchase a three-mile site in the Monaugium area of New Haven to build a $6-million resort. Plans were also made to erect a boardwalk along the three-mile stretch, several exclusive high-class restaurants and numerous concessions. The leader also considered purchasing nearby property that included a roller-skating rink and several houses in the East Haven Shoreline.

69. **"Daddy Grace to Use Fire Hose on 300,"** *New York Amsterdam News*, **July 28, 1956, p. 1.**

Daddy Grace baptized 300 followers in Harlem, New York, with a fire hose. The local ministers condemned this method of baptism. Because so many people were being baptized, Grace thought this was the best way to do it.

70. **"Daddy Grace Visits Charlotte,"** *Charlotte Observer*, **September 14, 1959, p. B-5.**

Daddy Grace visited Charlotte and an estimated crowd of more than 30,000 people watched the annual parade of Bishop Charles "Sweet" Daddy Grace and Charlotte's House of Prayer For All People. It was reported that during this parade, Bishop Grace threw candy to the thousands from under his royal canopy on his girl-laden float. From "Daddy's" float, Elder Melvin Adams of the Charlotte church called Grace the man who is heading the way to a better America. Adams told the onlookers, "Join him and find happiness." The parade watchers were happy, stated the writer.

71. **"Daddy Grace Will Stage Big Parade,"** *Charlotte Observer*, **September 7, 1958, p. 10.**

It was reported that Daddy Grace's annual parade in Charlotte for 1958 would be bigger than the previous year's (1957) parade. In 1957, Daddy Grace's throne was on the bed of a trailer truck, and three bands set a pace for the procession. The writer declared that the 1957 parade saw sidewalks packed with cheering and hand-clapping people as the fabled Black religious leader made his way through Charlotte.

72. **"Daddy Grace Warned: No Collections in Court,"** *Charlotte Obser-*
    ver, **January 3, 1958, p. B-1.**

    Mrs. Louvenia A. Royster, a retired school teacher from Georgia,
    charged in a Washington, DC, court that Bishop C. M. (Daddy) Grace
    married her in 1923 and deserted her in 1928. She requested that
    Grace be ordered to support her and her daughter. The bishop denied
    having married Mrs. Royster. Judge Alexander Holtzoff objected to the
    large groups of Grace's followers who gathered around the evangelist
    during recess periods in the courthouse halls. Judge Holtzoff also told
    Grace to stop accepting contributions from his followers in the Federal
    courthouse.

73. **"Daddy Grace Wins Case, Wasn't Married,"** *New York Amsterdam*
    News, **January 25, 1958, p. 1.**

    The court ruled that Bishop Grace was never married to Mrs. Louvenia
    A. Royster, who had sued him for nonsupport of her child. The judge
    ruled that Mrs. Royster did not prove her claim against Grace and
    dismissed the suit.

74. **"Daddy Grace's Deals,"** *New York Amsterdam News*, **September 9,
    1961, p. 11.**

    The newspaper printed the details of the property that Grace had
    purchased in New York City. There was a rider attached to the contract
    by which a group of white businessmen were able to get all of Daddy
    Grace's real estate holdings in New York for less than $2,000,000.

75. **"Daddy's Holding Worth $4 Million,"** *Charlotte News*, **June 15, 1960,
    p. 1.**

    According to the United States Tax Court, Bishop C. M. Grace was
    worth $4,064,739 on December 31, 1956. The House of Prayer For All
    People said the money and property belonged to the church and not to
    its leader personally. A year-long government investigation of Grace's
    finances showed he first became a millionaire in 1947 with his net worth
    listed at $1,128,668. The Bank of Charlotte (NC) was listed as having
    more of his money than any other single banking institution on that
    date. Reports showed that he had $111,110 in a savings account, and
    $330,000 in certificates of deposit. Other Charlotte banks with Grace
    funds on that date were Wachovia Bank and Trust, $131.00 in savings
    and $46,442 in checking account; Union National Bank, $30,668. His

total holdings in North Carolina banks on that date was $217,658, not including the $330,000 in certificates of deposit at the Bank of Charlotte.

76. **"15,000 See Daddy Grace Baptize Hundreds,"** *Pittsburgh Courier*, **August 26, 1950, p. 4.**

At least 15,000 persons witnessed the baptism of 208 people in Washington, DC, by Bishop C. M. (Daddy Grace). Titled "The Grace American Peace Parade," it included four brass bands, special armed Grace Police officers, guards and typical fanfare. It was believed that the Bishop's contention that the water from River Jordan was not needed may have been his response to the unique tanking of water from the Holy Land for a local baptism, by a contemporary religious organization, according to this article. The "Street Baptizing" was the beginning of the 16th session of the Twenty-Fourth Annual Holy Convocation. Bishop Grace, who admitted that he never knows what his message is going to be and that he preaches by the appointment of God, was highly elated at the success of the venture, concluded the reporter.

77. **"500 Daddy Grace Converts Dipped in Three Hours,"** *Afro-American*, **March 8, 1940, p. 1.**

It was pointed out that 500 new members of the United House of Prayer For All People in Washington, DC, were baptized in Benjamin Swimming Pool by Daddy Grace. Bishop Grace delivered the sermon prior to the dipping of the white-robed converts. The dipping took three hours. Members of the movement from churches in southwest Washington, Marshall Heights, Hall Hills, Alexandria, Arlington, and Anacostia attended the services and participated in the baptism and parade. . . .

78. **Gary, Kays. "Spiritual Life Not for Wife, So Daddy's Marriage Ended,"** *Charlotte Observer*, **January 13, 1960, p. 2.**

The writer states that Mrs. Marie Miller, a niece of Daddy Grace, from New Bedford, Massachusetts, said Daddy Grace was married and divorced. The wife, whom Mrs. Miller would not identify, still lived (in 1960) "somewhere in the United States." The marriage broke up years and years ago, "because his wife didn't want a spiritual life," according to Mrs. Miller. The union brought one son who was now dead, declared his niece.

79. **Gaultney, Judy. "House of Prayer Got Its Start in Downtown Tent,"** *Charlotte News*, **February 17, 1979, p. A-5.**

This religion writer states that the Charlotte United House of Prayer For All People started by Daddy Grace had its beginnings in a tent in 1926. The church in Charlotte was called the "Mother Church" for the Charlotte area. The organization claimed more than 13,000 members in Charlotte, concludes Gaultney.

80. **"Grace Cleared in Alimony Suit,"** *Standard-Times* **(New Bedford, MA), January 15, 1958, pp. 1, 5.**

The case against Daddy Grace for alimony and support by Mrs. Louvenia A. Royster, who claimed she married Grace in 1923 was dismissed in the United States District Court in Washington, DC, because she had not proven her claim. During the trial, Grace said, "I swear with my hand on the Bible that I never did such a thing."

81. **"Grace's Niece Asks Court Drop 'Widow' as Contestant,"** *Standard-Times* **(New Bedford, MA), February 3, 1960, p. 2.**

Bishop Grace's niece, Mrs. Marie Miller of New Bedford, Massachusetts, asked the Probate Court at Taunton to drop Mrs. Jennie L. Grace as a contestant to Bishop Grace's will because she had no legal standing as Grace was divorced from her. Mrs. Miller was left $10,000 in the will, while Mrs. Grace was left nothing in the will.

82. **"Grace's Personal Property Here Valued at $350,000,"** *Standard-Times* **(New Bedford, MA), January 29, 1960, pp. 1, 11.**

It was stated that personal property valued "conservatively" at $350,000 was left in New Bedford, Massachusetts, by the late "Bishop" Charles M. Grace. The personal property included cash, household furnishings and paintings. In some instances, Grace held property as trustee for the United House of Prayer For All People.

83. **"Grace's Street Baptism Irks Baptist Ministers,"** *Philadelphia Tribune*, **August 16, 1952, p. 6.**

This newspaper article stated that some Black Baptist Ministers in Philadelphia and surrounding areas would seek an injunction against Bishop Grace that would bar him from spraying his followers on the streets with fire hoses and calling it "baptism." The ministers said they consider Baptism sacred, and there was no Biblical foundation for the Bishop's mode of administering the rites.

84. **"'Heaven's New Owner Gives Blessing,"** *Washington Post*, **February 25, 1938, p. 20.**

This is a photo of Bishop Charles M. Grace giving benediction in his home in Washington, DC, to three female followers, whom it is said to number a million. It was also stated that the Bishop made a down-payment of $2,000 for the $20,000 building which was Father Divine's main "Heaven" in Harlem, New York. The writer called Grace a trustee of the House of Prayer For All People of Washington, DC, and Baltimore, Maryland.

85. **Herndon, Charles. "Daddy Grace to Use Fire Hose on 300,"** *New York Amsterdam News*, **July 28, 1956, p. 1.**

It was stated that some 4,000 followers of Bishop C. M. Grace met in Harlem, New York, for the 30th Annual Convocation of the House of Prayer. It was estimated that 300 persons would officially become members of the House of Prayer after they were baptized with a fire hose.

86. **Hicks, James L. "How White Firm Got Daddy Grace's Millions,"** *New York Amsterdam News*, **September 9, 1961, pp. 1, 11.**

Daddy Grace told his followers that when he bought property in New York City that he paid $18,000,000 for it. When he died, the former owners of the property declared that Grace had really paid only $4,000,000 for it.

87. **Hyams, Joe. "Daddy Grace Displays Faith of His Followers,"** *New York Herald Tribune*, **May 11, 1958, pp. 1, 17.**

The reporter interviewed Daddy Grace in his new home in Los Angeles, California. He asked the leader a number of questions. Grace told Mr. Hyams that "the man who drinks shall not inherit the Kingdom of Heaven." He was queried about the various properties that he and his church owned. Grace stated, "God owns it—everything." "Do you know how God came to America?" he was asked. "He came with me," replied the evangelist. Bishop Grace was asked about members of his congregation. He asserted: "If God can trust himself within me, they (his followers) can trust themselves with me. "Are you a prophet?" Hyams asked. "I can only say that if Moses came here now, he would have to follow this man," said Grace, pointing to himself.

88. _____. **"Daddy Grace Faithful Says He Cures the Sick, Raises the Dead, Charges Low Rent,"** *Standard-Times* **(New Bedford, MA), March 13, 1958, p. 11.**

The writer was a *New York Herald Tribune* reporter and visited Daddy Grace in Los Angeles, California, where Grace had just completed the purchase of a $500,000, 85-room mansion. The reporter said Daddy Grace declared, "They [his followers] give me money because they know I will make it multiply for them." When Grace was asked, "What do you do for converts?" he said, "Ask them." Some of his followers asserted that "He cures the sick." Others declared, "He makes the blind see, the lame walk, raises the dead, makes us prosper, and charges us low rent."

89. **"In Same Corner,"** *New York Age*, **February 11, 1950, p. 2.**

It was stated that former triple-title boxing champion Henry Armstrong joined Bishop Grace's House of Prayer in Los Angeles, California. This article declared that Armstrong would take to the road with Grace the same manner that ex-dancer Bill Bailey did to get experience in "fighting Satan." It was also pointed out that Daddy Grace had 301 churches in his chain.

90. **Johnson, Haynes. "Tax Men List 'Daddy's' Worth,"** *Washington Star*, **September 21, 1960, pp. C-1, C-19.**

It was pointed out that the Internal Revenue Service said that during the years 1945 to 1956 Daddy Grace "had under his exclusive control 90 bank and savings and loan accounts." It was stated that Daddy Grace's estate was valued unofficially at more than $25 million. Grace alone was authorized to draw checks on 71 of the 90 bank accounts, according to the IRS. Daddy Grace established at least 108 Houses of Prayer along the Eastern Seaboard, in the Midwest and in California, declared Johnson. It was in 1929 at Newport News, VA, that Daddy Grace promulgated the constitution and by-laws for the government of his church.

91. **Kelly, Tom. "Daddy's Riches Fall From Grace,"** *Washington Star*, **July 25, 1961, p. 4.**

Mr. Kelly asserted that in 1956, Daddy Grace took in over $4 million, yet according to the Internal Revenue Service records, Grace only reported $408.00. It was also surmised that Daddy Grace told his followers that he paid $18 million for the Elorada Towers in New York, yet he only paid something over $4 million—a disparity of $14 million. Three different groups were battling for Grace's property: one led by Walter McCullough of Washington, DC, who claims to be Grace's legal successor; another one headed by John W. McClure, also of Washington, DC, who claimed that Bishop McCullough's election was not legal since it violated the constitution of the church; and a third group, including white businessmen from New York City, who had been for years Bishop Grace's financial consultants. Most of Grace's followers were not too concerned about the outcome of the controversy. One of them said: "We are not concerned with which side wins. We are just watching and praying for Daddy himself to come back and straighten things out." The writer concluded that Daddy's finances were as obscure as the Book of Apocalypse but the McClure group was able to throw a little light on them, though not exactly a blinding light.

92. **Kilgo, John. "Daddy Still Sweet; Money Still Green,"** *Charlotte Observer*, **June 19, 1959, p. B-5.**

The reporter interviewed Daddy Grace while he was in Charlotte visiting the United House of Prayer For All People. Mr. Kilgo quoted Daddy Grace as declaring:

> I love Charlotte because I bore my cross here. I went to jail many times in Charlotte. . . . Some boys came in here sick and I gave them my toast and they were well.

It was pointed out that many of the Bishop's converts gave him money while he was eating in the dining room of the church. The writer also observed that Sweet Daddy Grace had a gold watch on his arm and a diamond-studded ring on his finger.

93. **Kuralt, Charles. "Daddy Grace: For Millions of U. S. Followers, He's New Prophet,"** *Charlotte News*, **August 16, 1956, p. B1.**

According to this writer, to some one million worshippers, Bishop Charles Emmanuel (Daddy) Grace is the Prophet Elijah come to prepare the way for the Lord. Mr. Kuralt declares that countless rival prophets—Father Divine, Prophet Jones, Bishop S. C. Johnson—have accused him of living in sin with his female "angels." "Lies," he shouts to his "children," and they shout back, "Amen." It was suggested that nowhere has "Sweet Daddy" built his Houses (of Prayer) on a more solid rock than in North Carolina. There are about 16 Houses of Prayer in the state, including Dallas, Mount Holly, Matthews, Greensboro, Salisbury, Winston-Salem, Lexington, etc. There are six in Charlotte. He apparently came to Charlotte in 1926 and started baptizing Blacks in a mudhole on Long Street in the middle of "Hell's Half Acre," the toughest section in the town. It was estimated that in 1956 there were about 13,000 members in Charlotte that were followers of Daddy Grace.

94. _____. **"Daddy Grace is Rough on Rivals,"** *Charlotte News*, **August 17, 1956, pp. B1, B12.**

Mr. Kuralt asserted that Daddy Grace had little respect for his rivals such as Bishop S. C. Johnson and Father Divine. It was reported that Daddy Grace said, "Father Divine is an imposter. He says he's God. Do you know what he really is? A lying, old fool. I dismiss him. Period." Daddy Grace's houses were managed by local elders in each of his 67 cities and towns. The elders were hand-picked by Grace. The Bishop observed, "You don't have to be a great man. You just have to be honest." When Grace came to Charlotte, he had his $25,000 bus converted into a diner on wheels, cruised the city beginning at dawn, picking up the ill and lame. And if any of the faithful were too poor to afford a feast, they were fed on the way to the church. While in Charlotte, Grace once asserted, "It's not my little crowd against our little crowd; the House of Prayer is for ALL people."

95. _____. **"Daddy Grace: Saviour or Fraud,"** *Charlotte News*, **August 18, 1956, p. B1.**

Mr. Kuralt apparently attended a church meeting at one of the Houses of Prayer in Charlotte, and he reported what he observed. At one meeting one of Grace's followers read a letter he had sent the church. Grace said: "Don't be foolish and ignore my teaching. You can't have excuses to hide behind. . . . Get your soul in order. . . ." It was signed with "much love to all my children." It was pointed out that Charlotte Police Chief Frank Littlejohn said, "The fellow (Daddy Grace) has got something—I don't know what. All I know is very few of his members ever come to Police Court." The reporter asked a local preacher what he thought of Grace, and the preacher replied: "He's a monster who is defrauding the people—but don't use my name please. I'd lose half my congregation." Ask the followers of Daddy what they think of him, and they'll sing it to you:

> "Daddy Grace is the only saviour,
> The world's chief cornerstone.
> "While he's with us, we'd better obey,
> The world will end when he's gone."

96. **MacDonald, Donald. "Memorial Is Held for (Daddy) Grace,"** *Winston-Salem (NC) Sentinel,* **January 12, 1961, pp. 1-2.**

Followers of the late Bishop C. M. (Sweet Daddy) Grace held a midnight mass in Charlotte, North Carolina, as a memorial to the Black religious leader who founded 350 congregations of the House of Prayer For All People. The mass at the red-white-and blue temple began at 12:05 am. on the 12th, a year to the minute from the time Daddy Grace died in Los Angeles, California. His followers have read symbolism into the last written words of this man who called himself "the boyfriend of the world." "Be ready," Bishop Grace wrote the secretary of the local House of Prayer on January 8. "I'm leaving on the 12th to fly from kingdom to kingdom."

97. **Miller, Sigsbee. "Thousands See Daddy Grace's Church Parade,"** *Charlotte Observer,* **September 12, 1949, p. 3.**

Mr. Miller reported that Daddy Grace led 5,000 followers in a traffic-stopping demonstration through Charlotte streets. Another 35,000 people stood on the sidewalks and watched the parade. According to the writer, the parade climaxed a week-long celebration of the Twenty-Third Holy Convocation week of the House of Prayer— traditionally one of the gaudiest, noisiest events of the year in North Carolina. It was also stated that a thousand white-robed baptismal candidates were baptized in a pool. At the end of the parade, Daddy Grace spoke to his followers. Grace declared: "Isn't this pretty? Heaven on earth, ain't it? . . . You can't follow but one man. Remember Moses?" His sermon was brief. Mr. Miller pointed out that Daddy Grace had recently purchased Father Divine's "Heaven" (church) in New York. Bishop Grace insisted that his 300 churches "have nothing in common" with the ideas of his competitor (Father Divine).

98.   **Morisey, A. A. "'Daddy' Grace Visits Flock, Crowd Shouts, Sings, Pays,"** *Winston-Salem (NC) Journal-Sentinel,* **May 4, 1952, p. 1.**

Daddy Grace visited his House of Prayer in Winston-Salem (NC) and spent 90 minutes. The leader preached while at the church. He's reported to have declared:

> How can you love God when you hate those here with you? . . . that's the truth unless it zigzags on the way. I give you the Bible, that's all I give you. . . . House of Prayer people got to be fair—no crookedness about nothing. . . . The God that answers by fire is the God for us to serve. . . .

He also talked about Elijah, who said he was a "House of Prayer Prophet," quoted the Bible, urged unity, and praised his own business successes, concluded Mr. Morisey.

99.   **Munn, Porter. "Daddy's Worth Costs Him $250 Gift,"** *Charlotte Observer,* **September 6, 1958, p. 1.**

The article mentions that Millie Johnson, treasurer of the Wilmington, North Carolina, United House of Prayer For All People came to Charlotte and had planned to give $250.00 that she collected from her church. After having received Daddy Grace's "condemnation," Mrs. Johnson left Daddy Grace's presence and took the $250.00 with her. The leader allegedly "condemned" her for trying to preach in the Wilmington area. The House of Prayer's creed forbids women to preach. Grace brought charges against Johnson for the missing money, according to Munn.

100.   **"Never Heard of 'Wife' Bishop Grace Says,"** *Standard-Times* **(New Bedford, MA), January 4, 1958, p. 9.**

Mrs. Jennie Grace of New Bedford, Massachusetts, alleged that she was married to Bishop C. M. Grace on February 13, 1907. Bishop Grace denied having married her. Mrs. Grace stated she never got a divorce from the Bishop. She said she had a boy, who later died, and a girl by the religious leader. Mrs. Grace's daughter also lived in New Bedford. Over the years, Mrs. Grace said she received little support money from the Bishop.

101. **Oberdorfer, Don. "Grace Meant 'Faith' to Followers,"** *Charlotte Observer,* **February 5, 1960, p. B-1.**

Mr. Oberdorfer declared that while the late Bishop Charles M. (Sweet Daddy) Grace didn't advertise himself as God, he didn't deny it either. According to this reporter, many of his followers believed he was. Grace so dominated the sect he founded that almost literally he was the faith, asserted the writer. The sect leader once said: "I never said I was God, but you can't prove to me I'm not." Many of his converts asserted that they believed in "the Father, the Son, the Holy Ghost and Bishop C. M. Grace." According to some of his close associates, Grace was not well-educated, nor did he like signing his name on legal documents. It was pointed out that several social scientists who studied the Grace movement and other cults consider the extreme religious ecstasy a form of escape from the drab and frustrating daily lives led by many of the followers. One person summed up Daddy Grace's movement this way:

> Members of the more orthodox churches may stand on the sidelines and sneer all they please, but the fact remains Bishop C. M. Grace had something to offer the humble people who gave him allegiance. And that obviously was something they could not get in any other denomination— respect and a sense of belonging. . . .

102. **Overbea, Luix. "Lengthy Funeral at Charlotte Finally Ends for Daddy Grace,"** *Winston-Salem (NC) Sentinel,* **January 19, 1960, p. 1.**

Mr. Overbea states that thousands of followers, city policemen, special policemen, funeral directors and onlookers wore themselves out for Bishop C. M. (Sweet Daddy) Grace, founder and leader of the House of Prayer For All People. Gathering or passing through his House of Prayer on McDowell Street, in a community soon to be redeveloped under a slum clearance program, people from every walk of life climaxed what was perhaps the longest funeral in North Carolina history. This funeral began at 6:03 p.m. Sunday at the Charlotte railroad station when Daddy Grace's body arrived in a glistening, expensive, copper casket and was rolled on to a 1960 Cadillac hearse, just purchased by the Alexander Funeral Home. It ended at 1:15 p.m. this morning when elders dismissed a dancing, crying, shouting throng of enthralled admirers, observed the writer. Mr. Overbea also said that to add to the drama of the scene, Daddy Grace preached his own funeral. This was not intentional, but Elder E. L. Green of Los Angeles, Calif., brought with him a tape recording of a sermon Bishop Grace preached there. He played it at 10 p.m. Throughout the entire two-day proceedings, people constantly marched around the church to view the body, sometimes as fast as 2,000 persons an hour when the crowd outside was too large to handle. There was never a moment that someone was not gazing at the body, according to the reporter.

103. _____. **"Sweet Daddy Arrives, Spreads Joy and Love,"** *Winston-Salem (NC) Journal*, **February 14, 1957, p. 1.**

Daddy Grace preached in Winston-Salem (NC) and told his followers:

> When I get to a place, God is there and the people are happy. If the people are not happy, God is not there, and you can't go to heaven . . . I'm preaching the last and everlasting gospel. This is Daddy Grace talking, and I dare anyone to dispute me.

He also declared:

> I'm here just because I love you. I love you, and because I love you I can do you no harm. I'm preaching the last gospel. The world is coming to an end soon, and only one religion will survive. . . .

The Bishop concluded: I'm not a hypocrite because I don't preach for salary. The Bible says, 'freely you have received, freely you give.'"

104. _____. **"'Sweet Daddy' Grace Dies at Age 78,"** *Winston-Salem (NC) Journal*, **January 18, 1960, pp. 1, 5.**

The writer recalls the many visits that Daddy Grace made to Winston-Salem, Charlotte and other North Carolina cities. Daddy Grace's last visit to Winston-Salem was September 3, 1958, as he was on his way to Charlotte. An entourage of followers trailed him. On that occasion, he wore a gold-colored formal, tails and pants with brilliant blue stripes. It is reported that Daddy Grace earned his name, Sweet Daddy, in this manner: "He always had with him candy or something sweet. When the fervor of a meeting was highest he would throw out this candy, one piece at a time. He would comment: "Daddy Grace loves his children. See how sweet I am to you. I am the only daddy who treats his children like this." Although Sweet Daddy never received an "income" from his church work, he did believe in collections, asserts the reporter. Many persons who have sued the bishop lost their cases, ranging from women claiming to be his wife to discontented followers. The cases against him were invariably thrown out. He even won a case from the U. S. government when he was charged with paying only $41 income tax on $190,000 income, concludes Mr. Overbea.

105. _____. **"Sweet Daddy Sets Overflow House Agog,"** *Winston-Salem (NC) Journal*, **September 4, 1958, p. 1.**

Bishop C. M. Grace visited his House of Prayer in Winston-Salem (NC) and spoke before an overflow audience. Several carloads of his followers—from Baltimore, MD, Washington, DC, and various parts of North Carolina—followed him to the Twin City. When a reporter arrived during dinner time, Sweet Daddy beckoned him to come forward. The reporter started to sit down, but was quickly reminded that he was not to do so. Daddy handed him a piece of dry, but thoroughly buttered toast out of which the bishop had taken a bit. This was blessed bread, the reporter learned later as he observed followers who jammed the kitchen scramble for pieces of this same bread. Some of the followers gave Daddy a dollar bill. One man paid $3. Men, women and children alike scrambled for each piece thrown out, concludes the reporter.

106. _____. **"Paternity Suit May Shake Kingdom of Daddy Grace,"** *Jet*, **January 9, 1958, pp. 18-19.**

Mrs. Louvenia A. Royster claimed Grace married her in 1923 and was the father of her 30-year-old daughter. Mrs. Royster was seeking alimony. Grace was reported to have been free from scandal for a quarter of a century before this suit came up.

107. **Pearson, Drew. "'Sweet Daddy's' Heir to Be Named,"** *Washington Post*, **April 7, 1962, p. D-23.**

Mr. Pearson pointed out that four hundred of Sweet Daddy Grace's followers gathered in Washington, DC, to vote on who will take over the affairs of the founder and Bishop of the House of Prayer For All People. The writer asserted that Grace came to the United States in 1903 from the Portuguese Cape Verde Island. According to the writer, Bishop Grace was a one-man rule and because of that, now, so many problems followed his death. The election would be by secret ballot since there was pressure on Grace's followers and fear of reprisal if they don't vote right. The reporter pointed out that the more than 100 Houses of Prayers started by Grace grew from a $39 House of Prayer in West Wareham, MA. The candidates to succeed Grace included Bishop Walter McCullough of Washington, DC, and Elder Henry Price, Pastor of a House of Prayer in New York City. McCullough won the election.

108. **Pearson, Harry. "Large Crowd Sees 'Daddy Grace,'"** *Winston-Salem (NC) Journal*, **January 18, 1960, p. 1.**

In Charlotte, North Carolina, thousands of reverent, well-dressed Blacks viewed Daddy Grace's remains at his House of Prayer For All People. The coffin's glass top allowed mourners to see "Daddy Grace," who was dressed in black and gold.

109. **Perry, Al. "Daddy Grace Had $600,000 in North Carolina, U. S. Says,"** *Winston-Salem (NC) Journal*, **June 17, 1960, p. 3.**

According to United States tax lawyers, Daddy Grace controlled bank deposits and property in North Carolina worth more than $600,000 at the end of 1956. The bank deposits were in at least 18 accounts at banks spread out from Charlotte to Elizabeth City. The bulk of Grace's money in North Carolina was in bank accounts and savings deposit certificates at Charlotte—some $518,000 at the end of 1956. According to Perry, in addition, there was $198.52 at Winston-Salem, $2,951 at Greensboro, $3,782 at High Point, $3,637 at Salisbury and $10,273 at Wilmington—plus accounts in three or four other cities.

110. _____. "'Daddy' Grace Tax Battle Seen," *Winston-Salem (NC) Journal*, **May 22, 1960, p. 3.**

Mr. Perry asserts that Grace's House of Prayer was working quietly but hard on plans to fight a multi-million dollar tax battle with the United States Government. The reporter states that less than three weeks after the bishop's death, the government filed liens for back taxes and interest totaling 5.9 million dollars. The case ranks as one of the largest single income tax claims in history. The House of Prayer contends that practically all the money in the scattered accounts is designated as belonging to the church and should not be taxable as Grace's personal income, states the reporter.

111. **Poinsett, Alex. "Farewell to Daddy Grace,"** *Ebony*, **Vol. 15, No. 6, April 1960, pp. 25-34.**

Dr. Poinsett surmises that Daddy Grace was as much an enigma in death as he was in life. Some praised him as a profound mystic. Others condemned him as a Cadillac-riding materialist whose extraordinary vision paralyzed the nickels, dimes and dollars of his flock into a 12-state, real estate and church empire said to be worth $25,000,000. Daddy Grace's real name was Marcilino Manuel Graca. He established more than 375 churches in 67 cities. Many of Daddy Grace's converts testified to the many miracles he performed for them, such as healing them and allowing them to have children after several miscarriages. The author asserts that, unlike many other cults, Grace did not frown on the use of cosmetics. Such materials, he contended, "help" magnify natural beauty if not used excessively. The author declared that Grace did look after his converts: (1) He established a pension fund for retired ministers and old, indigent members. (2) He provided a family association burial plan for his flock. (3) He built or bought, in every major town where a House of Prayer is located, multi-unit apartment buildings to house his church members. (4) In emergencies, he provided them with free food, clothing and shelter. Dr. Poinsett concluded:

> Although Bishop Charles M. (Sweet Daddy) Grace departed before he could balance his material accounts, the world will do the final bookkeeping on his moral ledger. Some will declare that he was one of "the greatest humanitarians who ever lived. Others will say, with equal conviction, "He was a colossal fraud. Only God can judge."

112. **"Police Link Grace with Gang-Style Murder of Elder Becton,"** *Color*, **September 1952, pp. 22-25.**

Rev. George Wilson Becton was murdered in Philadelphia on May 21, 1933, and one of Daddy Grace's followers was charged with the murder. Rev. Becton was seen as a threat to Daddy Grace in Philadelphia. Police failed to connect Grace to the murder.

113. **"Purple-Clad Daddy Grace Takes Stand,"** *Charlotte Observer*, **January 9, 1958, p. B-1.**

The article asserted that Daddy Grace took the witness stand in Washington, DC, and denied that he married Mrs. Louvenia A. Royster, a retired school teacher from Georgia. Mrs. Royster was suing Grace for alimony and support. She alleged that she married the evangelist in 1923 and he deserted her in 1928. Grace told inquiring reporters during a recess that there was no particular significance to his unusual attire that consisted of a black velvet collar worn over a purple cutaway. He also wore a bright chartreuse and black vest. A gold cross decorated his blue and yellow cravat.

114. **Rosenfield, Stephen S. "Daddy Grace Dies in Los Angeles, Cross Country Cortege Planned," *Washington Post*, January 13, 1960, p. B-2.**

The reporter states that Daddy Grace's kind of evangelistic, emotional spirituality made sinners weep and crowds chorus, "Yeah." He was flamboyant in his dress and manners, and a worldly wealth estimated in the millions of dollars. Mr. Rosenfield surmises that Daddy Grace's followers were intensely proud of all his accomplishments.

115. **"'Substantial' Cash Found in Grace's Estate Here," *Standard-Times* (New Bedford, MA), January 28, 1960, pp. 1,2.**

"Substantial" cash was found in New Bedford, Massachusetts at Bishop Grace's residence on County Street, which the evangelist occupied during his visits to this city. The amount of cash found by his administrators and New Bedford's city attorney was not disclosed.

116. **"Sweet Daddy's Sugar," *Newsweek*, Vol. 55, No. 7, February 15, 1960, p. 52.**

This article states that many of Daddy Grace's female "angels" could bear him out as he proclaimed himself "boyfriend of the world." It was also pointed out that the creed of the cult was set forth in a hymn to Grace, that goes:

> Daddy Grace is a holy prophet,
> An angel and a holy man.
> He has the key to the Kingdom,
> Has it always in his hand.

117. **"The Children Just Love Me and My House of Prayer!," *Afro-American*, October 22, 1949, p. 9.**

There is a photo of Bishop C. M. (Daddy) Grace playing a piano for some of his youthful followers at his home in Charlotte, North Carolina. This photo showed his carefully manicured fingernails and the very latest Parisian suit worn by the Bishop.

118. **Thomas, Phil. "Another Woman Claims To Be Daddy's Wife,"
Washington Star, January 3, 1958, p. B-4.**

It was pointed out that while Mrs. Louvenia A. Royster was suing
Daddy Grace for support and alimony, another woman, Mrs. Jennie
Grace of New Bedford, Massachusetts, also claimed to be Mrs. C. M.
Grace. Mrs. Grace sent a letter to Washington, DC, Federal District
Court to Judge Alexander Holtzoff stating that she was the Bishop's
first wife and that he "left me many years ago" after the birth of two
children. It was brought out in the article that Bishop Grace admitted
marrying a Jennie Grace at one time. Court papers also showed that
the evangelist married another woman in California in 1932. Attorney
Franklin Yasmer, who represented the leader, suggested that his
client was "a target, a sitting duck, for all kinds of claims." He
continued to explain: "He gets a lot of letters like this from women
who call him my spiritual husband, my heavenly husband. . . .
Women move into his home, and he has to throw them out."

119. _____. **"Bishop Grace Litigation Thickens as Third Group
Enters Case," *Washington Star*, August 3, 1961, p . B-1.**

Washington, DC., District Court Judge George L. Hart, Jr., appointed
Washington Attorney William B. Bryant as a court-appointed receiver
to straighten out the United House of Prayer For All People's "chaotic'
financial affairs that were left by Daddy Grace. Judge Hart stated that
the almost 40-year reign of Daddy Grace as Bishop of the 3-million
member religious group "was, in effect, a dictatorship run by one man"
who controlled all church funds under the organization's constitution.
Mr. Hart asserted:

> This is an effort to restore the church to the people . . . to
> protect the money that they saved . . . and let them go on
> their way. . . . This court has many things to do other than
> run churches, a task for which it is ill-prepared. . . .

120. _____. **"Daddy Grace Denies He Married in 1923,"
Washington (DC) Evening Star, December 29, 1957, p. A-14.**

Mrs. Louvenia A. Royster, a retired school teacher, claimed Daddy
Grace married her in 1923 and that she had a daughter by him in
1927. Grace was accused of deserting Mrs. Royster in 1928. The
cult leader denied all claims made by the plaintiff.

121. **"Uncle Sam Tells Daddy Grace: 'You Can't Take It with You,'"** *Washington News*, **February 1, 1960, p. C-1.**

    The United States Internal Revenue Service filed a $5,966,000 tax lien against the estate of Bishop C. M. (Daddy) Grace that amount represented unpaid taxes and interest for the years 1945 to 1956 according to the Internal Revenue Service. The writer declared that Grace was a colorful figure whose followers believed was divine and was distinguished by his six-inch fingernails that were painted vividly. He left the majority of his estate to the United House of Prayer For All People, which he founded. He left only $62,500 to his children and other relatives. His relatives filed suit in Massachusetts to break his will. It was also reported that Grace had $80,000 on his person when he died and that was missing. . . .

122. **"U. S. Investigates Status of Daddy Grace's Church,"** *Standard-Times* **(New Bedford, MA), February 17, 1960, p. 4.**

    Dana Latham, Internal Revenue Service Commissioner, informed a House Appropriations Subcommittee that the IRS filed a $5,990,648 tax lien against Bishop C. M. Grace's estate. It was also brought out that Grace had been under IRS examination for a long period of time. The IRS found that he had bank accounts in several states. Commissioner Latham wanted the answer to the following question: "Was the multimillion-dollar church founded by 'Sweet Daddy' Charles M. Grace an 'individual enterprise' rather than a recognized religious body?" The Commissioner was also concerned that the IRS received no assurance that Grace's holdings would be maintained intact for the protection of the government.

123. **"Was Daddy Grace Married or Was He Really at Sea?,"** *Charlotte News*, **January 2, 1958, p. 1.**

    This article is about Mrs. Louvenia A. Royster, 81, who sued Daddy Grace for nonsupport. She said she married Grace on September 26, 1923, in New York City when he used the name John Royster. She also alleged that she bore him a daughter. Mrs. Royster stated that Grace was running an employment-building and loan firm in Newark, New Jersey, at the time she married Grace. Bishop Grace said he was on the high seas on the day of the alleged wedding and denied knowing Mrs. Royster.

124. **Whiting, Albert N.   "From Saint to Shutter: An   Analysis of Sectarian Types,"** *Quarterly Review of Higher Education Among Negroes*, **Vol. 23, No. 4, October 1955, pp. 133-139.**

This article basically discusses the United House of Prayer For All People and its membership. The House of Prayer is a Christian sect of the holiness-charismatic variety, with the Bible as the sacred text. Dr. Whiting stated that this sect, led by Bishop "Daddy" Grace, believed in conversion, sanctification and the direct operation of the Holy Spirit through "gifts." It was particularly characterized by a set of beliefs to the effect that Bishop Grace was "God's man" and that his presence on earth was in line with the "Divine Plan" for the salvation of the worthy, namely all members of the House of Prayer.

125. **Wolfe, Thomas. "Women Collapse at Daddy's Bier,"** *Washington Post*, **January 21, 1960, p. B-1.**

Mr. Wolfe reported that in death as in life, Sweet Daddy Grace traveled first class when he was viewed by about 1,000 onlookers in Washington, DC. He was sealed in a $20,000 solid bronze casket with a glass cover. Elder Rives of California said Daddy Grace told him only a week before his death that he knew his days were numbered and that the other elders in the church should carry on his work.

126. **"Woman Names Daddy Grace,"** *Standard-Times* **(New Bedford, MA), December 21, 1957, pp. 1-2.**

Mrs.Louvenia A. Royster went into the United States District Court in Washington, DC, and claimed she married Charles M. Grace in 1923, who was then known as John H. Royster. She was a retired school teacher from Georgia suing Grace for support. Mrs. Royster said they were married in New York City. When she was in the courtroom, Bishop Grace looked at her, then turned to his lawyer and asked, "Who is she?"

127. **York, John. "Daddy Grace Attracts Throng of Faithful Despite Dust, Heat,"** *Charlotte Observer*, **September 10, 1954, p. B-1.**

Daddy Grace visited Charlotte, and people from as far away as California came to see him—and be present for the opening of Bishop Grace's new House of Prayer For All People. One convert was heard saying, "They can't condemn Daddy. They can't say he's wrong.

They're condemning the Bible." Daddy Grace preached at the church, and the church was packed. His followers would listen and sway to his words and chant their responses, declared the reporter.

128. _____. **"Sweet Daddy . . . 'He's Just Gone Away,'"** *Charlotte Observer*, **January 13, 1960, pp. 1-2.**

"Sweet Daddy's not dead; he's just gone away." That was the message at Sweet Daddy Grace's House of Prayer For All People in Charlotte, and a thousand followers heard it and wept and shouted. The author states, "It was a fitting requiem for a man who generated a fierce loyalty in those who followed where he chose to lead."

129. _____. **"The Spiritual Empire of Sweet Daddy Grace,"** *Charlotte Observer*, **February 20, 1983, pp. E-1, E-7.**

The writer declares that he doubts that the deaths of John F. Kennedy and Martin Luther King, Jr., caused more grief in some sections of Charlotte than that of Sweet Daddy Grace. It was stated that the annual Grace Holy Convocation Week in Charlotte drew upwards of 45,000 people from several states. He concluded:

When Sweet Daddy died, some of his people thought he would rise again in a few days, or perhaps on the anniversary of his death. He didn't make it. Others thought the world was doomed after his death. They may be proven right yet.

B. Shorter Articles About Daddy Grace

130. "'Bishop' Grace Purchases Former Synagogue Here," *Standard-Times* (New Bedford, MA), April 27, 1941, p. 3.

This article states "Bishop" Charles M. Grace, who worked as a cook here (New Bedford, MA) and sold patent medicine on Cape Cod before he became leader of the Church on the Rock of the Apostolic Faith, has purchased the former Ahavath Achim Synagogue at 55 Howland Street. . . ." No price was quoted for the purchase. It was also pointed out that before 1921 the "Bishop" was the Rev. Charles M. Grace, residing at 174 Smith Street and ministering to the congregation of the House of Prayer on Kempton Street near Cottage Street. According to this article, Grace claimed to have been elected a bishop in Boston in 1921 when the Church Founded on the Rock of Apostolic Faith was incorporated. . . . Bishop Grace's rise in the church affairs was meteoric. He soon became a rival of Father Divine and finally displaced Divine in the allegiance of many Harlem citizens, concludes the writer.

131. "Daddy Grace: Grandiloquent Negro Preacher Has a Half-Million Faithful Followers," *Life*, Vol. 19, No. 14, October 1, 1945, pp. 51-56, 58.

It was stated that Daddy Grace had been head of the Church on the Rock of the Apostolic Faith, sometimes called the United House of Prayer for All People, for 19 years. His followers declared, "We believe in God the Son, God the Holy Ghost and Bishop C. M. Grace as our leaders." In 1945 it was said that there were 500,000 members in 100 Houses of Prayers from Florida to Massachusetts. The writer declared that Grace said he arranged for World War II to end and his converts believed him. Bishop Grace was against smoking, drinking, war adultery. The article concluded:

> Though hardly a conventional Christian, Daddy Grace preaches Christian principles and promises his "saints" salvation if they will follow him. In turn, they trust him completely, write such things as "I praise the Lord for Daddy Grace because, through him, my soul has been abundantly blessed."

132. **Glasser, Barry. "Cape Verdeans: The People Without A Race,"** *Sepia*, **Vol 24, No. 11, November 1975, pp. 68-69.**

The author pointed out that Bishop Charles M. ("Sweet Daddy Grace"), who turned from dishwashing to founding the House of Prayer For All People, Inc., had about 3,000,000 followers between the 1930s and the 1950s, had approximately $25 million in assets at the time of Sweet Daddy's death in 1960.

133. **MacDonald, Donald. "Daddy Grace's Influence Keeps Growing,"** *Charlotte Observer*, **September 12, 1949, p. B-1.**

Mr. MacDonald reported that Bishop Grace's avowed purpose for starting his church occurred in Newport News, Virginia, in July 1929. The purpose was:

> To establish, maintain, and perpetuate the doctrine of Christianity and the Apostolic Faith throughout the world among all people; to erect and maintain Houses of Prayer and worship where all people may gather, irrespective of denomination or creed, and to maintain the Apostolic Faith of the Lord and Savior, Jesus Christ.

The church called for a Bishop and a Prophet, which offices Daddy Grace held. As Bishop, Grace had authority to ordain ministers; general control and supervision of their actions; ownership of all property for use and benefit of his congregation. He saw himself as God's Chosen One for all his flock. It was pointed out that the Bishop enjoyed all music—band music, organ music, and the boppish, ear-pounding music of his Royal Serenaders. He wondered by religious music must be morbid. Why, he would ask, should the Devil have all the good times? observed the writer. MacDonald said Grace advocated and preached Christian marriages among his churchmen. The reporter concluded: ". . . When examined, the House of Prayer services basically is little different from that of Holy Rollers."

134. **Roberts, Ric. "Born in Portugal, He Has Spread His Gospel Over World,"** *Pittsburgh Courier,* **September 17, 1949, p. 13.**

Roberts asserts that Bishop Grace was the great leader of a special diplomatic unit of French-Portuguese hosts and official guests of French Government. His followers contend that Grace was chosen "by appointment of God" to stand apart from all mortals. He is reported to have about 300 churches in the United States. The author declares that some reports stated that Daddy Grace had more than two million followers. According to officials of the Grace organization, there were more than 25,000 Grace followers in New York City; 25,000 in Newport News, Virginia; 10,000 in Norfolk, Virginia, and 130,000 in thirty-one North Carolina cities. There were some thirty-six establishments in Georgia, led by a total of some 25,000 members in Savannah where the Bishop owned a palatial summer residence.

C. Articles Providing Background Information

135. **"A Large-Sized Bust of Charles Emmanuel Grace,"** *Standard Times* **(New Bedford, MA), August 15, 1943, p. 2.**

A large-sized bust of Charles Emmanuel Grace was made by the famous Portuguese sculpture Agostino Roderigues. The work of art was carved in white Vermont marble weighing two tons. The dimensions of the bust were 46 inches high by 30 inches wide. There is also a picture of the bust of Bishop Grace and Mr. Roderigues in the newspaper.

136. **"A Sad, Old House Falls as Era Ends,"** *Standard-Times* **(New Bedford, MA), December 2, 1963, pp. 1, 10.**

Bishop Charles Emmanuel Grace's palatial home on Country and Parker streets in New Bedford, Massachusetts, was torn down to make way for construction of the new Parker Street School.

137. **"Accounts Filed in Estate of "Sweet Daddy" Grace,"** *Standard-Times* **(New Bedford, MA), January 8, 1964, p. 33.**

The second and third accounts in the estate of Bishop Charles Emmanuel Grace were filed in Taunton (New Bedford, MA) with the Register of Probate. The gross estate was estimated at $5,700,375.96 when first account was allowed. The second and third accounts listed $10,000 for Benjamin Grace, a brother; $564.18 for Ernest P. Taylor, an appraiser in California, where the evangelist had real estate holdings, an oil bill and charges from the City of New Bedford for Grace's tomb.

138. **Allen, Everett S.   "A Rainy Day in Harlem Proved "Daddy" Grace's Hold on His Followers,"** *Standard-Times* **(New Bedford, MA), January 17, 1960, p. 8.**

This reporter states:

> [In] 1953, Mr. Allen accompanied "Bishop" Charles Manuel Grace, founder of the House of Prayer for all People at the outset of the latter's annual "convocational" tour of the nation. This tour included stops at each House of Prayer, all the way from New Bedford to Atlanta and across the country to the West Coast.   Each visit was marked by "preaching testimony," climaxed by mass baptisms. The following eyewitness account, possibly the first of its kind, describes the visit to New York City's Harlem.   It portrays Grace's personal magnetism, love of showmanship, and devotion of his thousands of followers.

139. **"Amazing 'Daddy' Grace Lived by the Dollar,"** *Jet,* **Vol. 61, No. 8, November 5, 1988, p. 37.**

It was surmised that Daddy Grace follower's were literally mesmerized by his magnetic personality. Before his death in 1960 (January 12), Daddy Grace had acquired real estate across the country valued at $25,000,000, including some of the most expensive and prestigious addresses in New York City, even though he often called money "the root of all evil."

140. **"Bishop Grace Again Pointed Out as Mrs. Royster's Husband,"** *Standard-Times* **(New Bedford, MA), December 24, 1957, p. 6.**

Bishop Grace was pointed out again in United States District Court as the one-time husband of Louvenia A. Royster, who claims they were married in New York in 1923. It was also stated that Bishop Grace, alias John Royster, also went by the name James Morris.

141. **"Bishop Grace Buys New York Property, Value $4,700,000,"** *Standard-Times* **(New Bedford, MA), July 30, 1953, p. 16.**

Bishop Grace purchased an apartment building overlooking Central Park in New York City for $4,700,000. He purchased it on behalf of the United House of Prayer For All People. Trusteeship was vested in Grace. It was stated that the purchase was in the nature of an investment and that the building would continue to be used as an apartment.

142. **"Bishop Grace Controversy,"** *Standard-Times* **(New Bedford, MA), January 4, 1958, p. 9.**

Mrs. Jennie Grace of 352 Smith Street of New Bedford, Massachusetts, alleged that she married Charles M. Grace on February 13, 1909. Mrs. Grace displayed a certificate of marriage between herself and Charles M. Grace. The 65-year-old woman declared she never was divorced from Bishop Grace and has a daughter by the Bishop. The daughter, Mrs. Irene Noriega, also lived in New Bedford at 475 Purchase Street. There are photos of the two ladies in this article.

143. **"Bishop Grace Goes to Court,"** *Standard-Times* **(New Bedford, MA), December 20, 1957, p. 2.**

This article surmises that Bishop C. M. Grace, 74, went on trial in Federal District Court in Washington, DC, on charges by Mrs. Louvenia A. Royster that they were married in 1923. Mrs. Royster filed the suit in 1954 and asked for support for herself and a 30-year old daughter. Grace denied the charges.

144. **"Bishop Grace Takes Stand, Denies He Wed Mrs. Royster,"** *Standard-Times* **(New Bedford, MA), January 9, 1958, p. 20.**

Bishop Grace denied he ever married Mrs. Louvenia A. Royster, a retired school teacher, from Georgia. Mrs. Royster testified that she and Grace were married in 1923 and he deserted her in 1928. The school teacher declared that Grace had once gone by the name John Royster and that he married her under that name. The trial took place in Federal District Court in Washington, DC. Grace's attorney asked him if he had ever married Mrs. Royster, and Grace replied, "I swear with my hand on the Bible that I never did such a thing."

145. **"Bishop Grace to Live Here,"** *Standard-Times* **(New Bedford, MA), April 17, 1943, p. 6.**

Bishop Grace paid $20,000 for the home of Mr. and Mrs. Pemberton H. Nye, located at 709 County Street, New Bedford, Massachusetts. Grace stated that this would be his personal residence in New Bedford and he would keep a staff of servants there at all times. The leader declared: "My work here made it necessary for me to buy a house, as I plan to hold church services soon in the synagogue which I purchased for that reason." He continued to say:

> Because my home is here now, I will be here often, but I still must be away much of the time to care for my flock in my 150 churches located up and down the Atlantic seaboard.

The 14-room house was built about 1843.

146. "'Bishop' Grace Will Allowed," *Standard Times* (New Bedford, MA), June 17, 1961, p. 3.

The will of Bishop Grace was allowed for probate in New Bedford Probate Court on June 16, 1961. Probate Judge Walter L. Considine appointed Attorneys Roy F. Teixeira and Rosalind Poll Brooker as administrators "with the will annexed." Attorneys Alfred J. Gomes, Lawrence Luny and William V. Reed stated at the probate hearing that they were witnesses to Daddy Grace's signing of the will.

147. "'Bishop' Grace's Body Interred," Standard-Times (New Bedford, MA), October 29, 1964, p. 5.

The body of Bishop Grace was moved from a $5-a-month city burial vault in New Bedford, Massachusetts to a newly-constructed marble tomb at Pine Grove Cemetery in New Bedford. Daddy Grace's body had lain in the rented vault for more than four years. He died January 12, 1960.

148. "'Bishop' Left Near $1 Million: Administrators File Inventory of Estate," *Standard-Times* (New Bedford, MA), August 8, 1961, pp. 1, 3.

The late Bishop Charles M. Grace left personal property valued at $399,277.10 and real estate worth $583,553. The inventory filed by his co-administrators showed that $252,053.77 was in a checking account on deposit in New Bedford, Massachusetts, and $23,331.22 on deposit in the same bank, the Merchants National Bank.

149. **"Bishop's Agent Is Fined $50 for Violation,"** *Winston-Salem (NC) Journal,* **January 3, 1949, pp. 1, 2.**

Rev. R. S. Stephen, a real estate agent for Bishop Grace, was fined $50.00 for failing to provide adequate toilet facilities for an apartment house owned by Bishop Grace. The four-apartment building in Winston-Salem was occupied by 22 people. Witnesses testified that repeated efforts had been made over a four-month period to get Stephen to make the required replacements. Even after he was arrested November 1 and told that he must remedy the situation, he continued to ignore the warnings, witnesses said.

150. **Booker, Simon. "Washington Notebook,"** *Ebony,* **Vol. 36, NO. 4, February 1981, p. 25.**

Mr. Booker declares that, in the 1920s and 1930s:

. . . Sweet Daddy Grace was a colorful religious figure who attracted hordes of reporters to street baptisms with water supplied from fire hydrants or with tours of his expansive midtown DeeCee edifice. Sweet Daddy started the United House of Prayer in tents and storefronts and in some cities was falsely labeled as a charlatan who socked it to poor folk and greedily extracted their limited pennies.

Mr. Booker also asserts what a difference a few years can make. Black cultists and divine religious characters who ride in Cadillacs and at the snap of fingers can produce a ghetto miracle are now almost an extinct species. This image of the soul stirrers was always false, according to the Hon. W. McCullough who rides out the storm in a trip best supplied by the catchy phrase, "from the storefront to the forefront." As successor to the original Sweet Daddy, the tall exciting pulpiteer in 1980 celebrated his 20th year, capping two decades of excellence. Unlike Sweet Daddy, the bishop found few fourth estaters tramping to his church doors loaded down with pen and pad or TV cameras, states the writer.

Booker concludes:

What the Bishop had done wasn't exactly the notorious kind of Black news. After his inspirational trek, he was an ignored pioneer. His two-decade stretch of saving souls in the city's most downtrodden areas reads like the Bible parable of fish and the loaves of bread, a one-man religious HUD which hit pay dirt during some hard lean years.

The author also declares that while Bishop McCullough was no show biz character by any means, he is as worthy of news media coverage for his wonderful decades of excellence as was the late Sweet Daddy Grace.

151. **"Boston Lawyer Retained by Grace's Widow Here,"** *Standard-Time* **(New Bedford, MA), January 22, 1960, p. 4.**

Mrs. Jennie L. Grace and her daughter, Mrs. Irene Noriega, of New Bedford, retained Attorney Ray Teixeira to represent them in the estate of Bishop Charles M. Grace. During Grace's lifetime, several women claimed that they had married him at one time or another. Mrs. Jennie L. Grace produced a marriage certificate in 1958 of her 1909 marriage to Daddy Grace. Pre-trial papers in the Washington, DC, 1958 trial court showed that Daddy Grace admitted to marrying Jennie Grace. There were reports of a divorce but Mrs. Grace claimed no papers were ever served on her, concluded the writer.

152. **"By the Appointment of God,"** *Pittsburgh Courier,* **August 26, 1950, p. 4.**

This article stated that fifteen thousand people saw Bishop C. M. Grace again utilize special equipment of the Washington, DC, fire department to baptize 208 followers. There is a photo of the bishop and most of the 208 people that were sprayed with water from the fire department. This event was part of the annual mass baptism that was sponsored each August by Grace.

153. **"County Street Home Sold to Bishop Grace,"** *Standard Times* **(New Bedford, MA), April 15, 1943, p. 2.**

This article asserts that the 14-room residence of Mr. and Mrs. Pemberton H. Nye, located on County Street between Parker and Pope Streets, in New Bedford, Massachusetts, was purchased by Bishop Charles M. Grace to be used for his residence. There is also a picture of this house.

154. **"County Won't Sue Grace Sect,"** *Charlotte Observer,* **June 30, 1964, p. 1.**

The Mecklenburg (NC) County Commissioners, rather than face a nebulous battle in court, agreed to offer $17,250 for some of the property of the late Daddy Grace. Hamlin Wade, who handles some of the county's legal matters, told commissioners of a problem in trying to condemn the property at the southeast corner of Third and McDowell streets. "We don't know exactly who to sue," he said. He explained that Daddy Grace, the leader of a religious sect, died in 1960 and left the property to the "House of Prayer and all the people in it." Wade said the organization was, in effect, a corporation but that he could find no corporate charter, concluded the writer.

155. **"Court Bars Outside Bid for Daddy Grace Assets,"** *Washington Post*, **June 9, 1960, p. B-1.**

District Court Judge Edward A. Tamm of Washington, DC, ruled that assets of the late Sweet Daddy Grace would not be collected in Washington, DC, by any outsider from the state of Massachusetts. Judge Tamm stated that if he ruled that Bristol County, Massachusetts, had a claim to Daddy Grace's assets in Washington, DC, then his estate would not be subjected to $758,853 in Washington, DC, income and estate taxes. Judge Tamm also appointed the National Bank of Washington to collect the assets and hold them for court-directed distribution.

156. **"Court Ousts Daddy Grace Successor, Names Lawyer and Church Receiver,"** *Washington Post*, **August 25, 1961, pp. B-1, B-2.**

Daddy Grace's successor, Walter McCullough, was removed from his official position as head of the United House of Prayer For All People by Washington, DC, District Court Judge George L. Hart, Jr. Judge Hart appointed Washington Attorney William B. Bryant as receiver of all church funds and church property. Mr. Hart ordered McCullough not to destroy or exercise control over any church records, nor transfer any church funds. The judge directed Mr. Bryant to take over the church property and preserve its assets, determine who are members of the church in good standing and report to the court on the direction of the church during Daddy Grace's lifetime. Under the church constitution, Bishop Grace had complete control of all church affairs, including cash deposits, real estate and other investments.

157. **Covington, Roy.   "Daddy Grace Parade Brings Joy to S. McDowell Street,"** *Charlotte Observer*, **September 9, 1957, p. 1.**

Daddy Grace was in Charlotte and led a parade down South
McDowell Street. The parade was the feature of the Thirty-First "Holy
Convocation of the United House of Prayer" of which Grace was the
founder, organizer and Lord Master. From his throne on the bed of
a trailer truck, surrounded by his coterie of "angels" Daddy Grace let
his benevolent glance sweep the throng as he rode along. One
follower observed:

> When he (Daddy Grace) comes, everybody just comes in
> from miles and miles around. You know how it is, this time
> of year, all the little mission branches gotta' flow together into
> the big river.

158. **"Daddy Grace Builds 20-Unit Dwelling in Newport News (VA),"**
      ***Afro-American*, June 18, 1949, p. 6.**

There is a photo of Bishop C. M. (Daddy) Grace entertaining members
of the Newport News City Council at a luncheon in the dining room of
the new 20-family apartment house recently built by the House of
Prayer in that city. The building cost about $140,000. Bishop Grace
said his church was endeavoring to help provide more and better
housing for Black people throughout the country.

159. **"Daddy Grace Buys $46,000 Sanctuary,"** *Jet*, **December 8, 1955,**
      p. 21.

Daddy Grace purchased the old Empress Theater in Columbus, Ohio,
for $46,000 cash. He turned the theater into a church.

160. **"Daddy Grace Buys $72,000 Mansion in Monticlair, New Jersey,"**
      ***Afro-American*, November 7, 1953, pp. 6, 20.**

The leader purchased a mansion in Montclair, New Jersey, for
$72,000. Many of the white people in this exclusive suburb were
upset about the purchase because Grace had planned to paint his
estate red, white, and blue. The local residents thought that their
property value would go down when Grace moved in, stated the
reporter.

161. **"Daddy Grace Buys Tallest N. Y. Apartment House, Etc.,"** *Jet*,
      May 21, 1953, p. 20.

Daddy Grace bought the tallest New York Apartment House, named the "Eldorado" for an estimated $4,000,000. The building was 34-stories high and had 216 apartments in it.

162. **"Daddy Grace Cult Joins Estate Fight,"** *Washington Post*, **June 10, 1960, p. B-2.**

A group of lay members of the United House of Prayer For All People joined a long list of claimants for the estate of Sweet Daddy Grace in a District Court in Washington, DC. The congregation members learned after Grace's death that money given in the name of the House of Prayer found its way into the Grace estate. The members also asked for an order restraining Grace's successor, Bishop Walter McCullough, from dispensing any of the funds left by Grace pending a court hearing. Attempts to gather the estate's assets were also under way in 14 states as well as in Cuba.

163. **"Daddy Grace Denies Marriage to D. C. Woman,"** *Jet*, **May 10, 1956, p. 16.**

Grace denied marrying Mrs. Louvenia A. Royster in 1923. She filed suit against him for alimony. Mrs. Royster said Grace was the father of her daughter.

164. **"Daddy Grace Estate Fights Tax Lien,"** *Washington Evening Star*, **April 14, 1960, p. C-4.**

The Internal Revenue Service sought back taxes and penalties totaling $5.9 million from the estate of the late Bishop Daddy Grace. Attorneys for Grace's United House of Prayer For All People protested against the IRS claim. They argued that Grace held property only as leader of the House of Prayer and this was not his personal property. The attorneys also argued that all tax deficiencies in the 1945-1955 period were excused by the statute of limitations.

165. **"Daddy Grace Estate Row Irks Judge,"** *Washington Post*, **July 29, 1960, p. B-1.**

District Court Judge George L. Hart, Jr., of Washington, DC, postponed a hearing on a request by Bishop Walter McCullough, Daddy Grace's successor to stop a "splinter group" led by James Walton of Philadelphia from using the United House of Prayer For All

People's name. Mr. Walton's suit asked that Bishop McCullough be restrained from spending any church money until the court held a full hearing. It charged that contributions from the congregation of the church had wound up in Grace's personal estate.

166. **"Daddy Grace Group Wins Church Name Suit,"** *Washington Star*, **October 17, 1960, p. B-1.**

Judge George L. Hart, Jr., of the District Court of Washington, DC, ordered James Walton of Philadelphia to stop using the name of the late Charles M. Sweet (Daddy) Grace's church. Mr. Walton alleged that Daddy Grace and his followers had abandoned use of the name several years ago. A number of suits were brought against Daddy Grace's successor, Bishop William McCullough, and the United House of Prayer For All People following the death of Bishop Grace.

167. **"Daddy Grace Guard Fined,"** *Charlotte Observer*, **October 9, 1958, p. 10.**

Mr. Earl Richmond, a bodyguard for Bishop Daddy Grace, was fined $50.00 in Raleigh (NC) and given an 18-month suspended sentence. He was charged with three charges of assault with a deadly weapon. The assault charges were brought following a shooting incident, September 8, near Daddy Grace's church in Raleigh.

168. **"Daddy Grace in New York City for Indefinite Stay,"** *New York Amsterdam News*, **May 7, 1958, p. 5.**

Daddy Grace visited his churches in the Greater New York Metropolitan and New England areas and stated he would stay for an indefinite period of time. Bishop Grace presided over some of the church services while he was in the area.

169. **"'Daddy' Grace Increases Property Holdings from California to Dixie,"** *Afro-American*, **June 18, 1949, p. 6.**

It was stated that Bishop Grace built a House of Prayer in Baltimore that cost $130,000. He had churches from New England to Florida and some states in the Middle West and Far West. There was, for example, a $40,000 church in Los Angeles. This article pointed out that the Bishop conferred recently with the mayor and chief-of-police in Charlotte about permitting Black taxi cabs in that city. They said that would be done if possible.

170. **"Daddy Grace Land Sold to County,"** *Charlotte News*, **June 30, 1964, p. B1.**

It was pointed out that the Mecklenburg County Commissioners wanted to buy the land that the United House of Prayer For All People was located on, but the problem was that they couldn't separate Bishop C. M. (Sweet Daddy) Grace's affairs from those of his church. The county attorneys were having problems finding out who to sue to get title to church property. It was left by Sweet Daddy to the House of Prayer, Inc., when he died, but "There's no such animal," said Attorney Hamlin Wade, who represented the county.

171. **"Daddy Grace Safe Yields Records of $900,000,"** *Washington Post*, **March 19, 1960, p. B-1.**

A safe in Charlotte, North Carolina, showed evidence of $900,000 in bank deposits belonging to the late C. M. Grace. The safe contained a letter telling of an income tax refund of $4,069.33 which was never claimed. There was also letters containing gifts of money and deeds to property in the Carolinas.

172. **"Daddy Grace Tagged by Mrs. Royster As Her Husband,"** *Afro-American*, **December 28, 1957, p. 1.**

Mrs. Louvenia A. Royster, a school teacher from Georgia, claimed that Daddy Grace was married to her and sued him for support of her daughter. She alleged that they were married in 1923. Daddy Grace denied he ever married her.

173. **"'Daddy' Grace Tomb Planned,"** *Standard-Times* **(New Bedford, MA), February 20, 1960, p. 4.**

It was reported that Daddy Grace's relatives planned to bury him in a mausoleum at Oak Grove Cemetery in New Bedford, Massachussetts. Before a mausoleum could be built, it first had to have the approval of the local cemetery board. Mrs. Marie J. Miller, a niece of Daddy Grace, from New Bedford, reserved a lot in the cemetery for the tomb.

174. **"Daddy Grace's Cuban Paradise,"** *Ebony*, **Vol. 9, No. 1, November 1953, pp. 86-90.**

It was stated that, in 1936, Grace purchased Finca Zorillo, a sumptuous country estate and fruit farm that had once been the home of the Minister of the Interior of Cuba. He renamed it Finca Gracioso. The article asserted that Daddy Grace knew most of the influential people of Cuba and had audiences with President Fulgencio Batista and called upon the American Consul. The farm harvested limes, lemons, mangos, bananas, coconuts and papayas. The estate was valued at more than $100,000. It was also pointed out that last year (1952) Grace had acquired the Elorado, New York's tallest apartment hotel on swank Central Park West for an estimated $4,000,000.

175. **"Daddy Grace's Fabulous Fingernails,"** *Hue*, **November 1956, pp. 12-15.**

Bishop Grace claimed his four-inch long fingernails were his sign of immortality because nobody else can grow them as long. He was asked why he never clipped his nails, and he said: "As Noah was before the flood, so is Daddy Grace before the fire." It was stated that his fingernails were probably the world's longest and gaudiest. . . .

176. **"Daddy Grace's House Brings $239,000,"** *Charlotte Observer*, **September 11, 1968, p. B1.**

The Charlotte Redevelopment Commission has purchased Daddy Grace's House of Prayer For All People for $230,000. The red, white, and blue church was built in 1956 for a reported $300,000 by the late Bishop C. M. "Sweet Daddy" Grace, ruler of the sect.

177. **"Daddy Grace's House of Prayer Tackles the Housing Problem in Several Cities,"** *Afro-American*, **June 18, 1949, p. 6.**

It was stated that Father Divine was not the only religious leader acquiring property in the 1940s. Daddy Grace was also buying up property. He purchased a 20-unit dwelling in Newport News, VA. A new House of Prayer Church was built in Augusta, GA, a few months ago. The leader was also building four apartments in Greer, SC. Each building cost about $10,000.

178. **"Daddy Grace's Religious Parade Set for Sunday,"** *Charlotte Observer*, **September 5, 1947, p. B-1.**

Between 5,000 and 10,000 followers of Daddy Grace were expected to participate in a huge religious parade in Charlotte. Bishop Grace spoke with an *Observer* reporter while he was in Charlotte. Unlike Father Divine, Daddy Grace stated that he does not claim to be the Almighty. The religious leaders asserted: "I am a just prophet—the prophet that Daniel saw in a vision. . . . The (his) background doesn't matter. Going forward, that is what counts." Asked about his age, Grace replied: "That's liking asking, 'How Old is Noah?'" It was also pointed out that Grace had a truck-trailer parked in front of the House of Prayer nightly during his stay. It had a modern refrigerating system which manufactured ice cream and kept soft drinks cool. Both were sold to his followers, as well as "Grace Loyal Vitamin." Grace was reported to have had 180 Houses of Prayers in the nation. He claimed to also have a half-million followers.

179. **"Daddy Grace's Successor Wins,"** *Washington News*, **October 17, 1960, p. B-1.**

District Judge George L. Hart, Jr., of Washington, DC, signed an injunction against Rev. James Walton of Philadelphia and ordered him to stop using the name, United House of Prayer For All People and also to stop interfering with meetings or harassing Bishop Walter McCullough, Daddy Grace's successor. Mr. Walton stated that he does not object to Bishop McCullough as spiritual successor to Bishop Grace, but questions the handling of church funds, concluded the article.

180. **"'Daddy' Grace's Taxes A Sweet $1.9 Million,"** *Washington Post*, **June 2, 1961, p. 1.**

The Internal Revenue Service settled its claim with Daddy Grace's estate for $1.94 million. The government said everything had been straightened out and that it found documents that showed what was Daddy Grace's personal property and what belonged to his churches. In his will, Bishop Grace left most of his estate to the United House of Prayer For All People. Ironically, the government was getting ready to sue him at the time of his death, claiming he owed back taxes from 1945 through 1956.

181. "D. C. Eyes Taxes, Claims Daddy Grace Lived Here," *Washington Evening Star*, April 14, 1960, p. C-4.

The Washington, DC, District ruled that Daddy Grace's legal residence was in that city and not in Bristol County, Massachusetts. Therefore, that county had no legal claim to Grace's property in Washington, DC. Bristol County alleged that Grace was a legal residence of that county and that it wanted to tax his estate. This article also pointed out that a woman who said she was Grace's widow also contested his will in Massachusetts.

182. "D. C. Ministers Crackdown on Daddy Grace," *Pittsburgh Courier*, August 9, 1949, p. 3.

This article stated that ten Black clergymen of Washington, DC, appealed to the Board of Commissioners. They asked the city fathers not to grant permission to Daddy Grace to use a city fire hose to baptize Grace's converts. Grace's spokesman said this ritual had been going on in Washington since 1933. It was pointed out that this ritual was a necessary adjunct to the ceremony looked forward to by the 400 converts recruited from Washington, DC, Maryland and Virginia and without it the cult would lose "face" with many potential converts. The annual event gave them something to look forward to——having their sins washed away by a fire hose, concludes the writer.

183. Dempsey, William K. "Bishop Grace Invites All Clergymen Here Meet with Him at His Church to End War," *Standard-Times* (New Bedford, MA), July 27, 1951, pp. 1, 4.

Daddy Grace was addressing his followers of the House of Prayer For All People in New Bedford (MA), he said, "Bring all the preachers here if you want to end the war." He told the audience, "anything God offers to you, I got it," referring his listeners to "Daddy Grace's combination safe." According to the reporter, Daddy Grace said nearby residents complained to the police that the loudspeaker system disturbed the peace. The Bishop declared: "A lot of people are stirred up . . . Why? Maybe because a lot of blankets are coming off faces because of my preaching." Later Daddy Grace referred to the complainants and asserted: "Why don't they come in and sit down and talk? That's Christianity."

184. "Died: Charles Manuel (Daddy Grace)," *Time*, Vol. 75, No. 4, January 25, 1960, p. 90.

It was stated that Daddy Grace died of a heart attack in Los Angeles. Before he died, according to the article, Grace had a coffee plantation in Brazil, a chicken farm in Cuba, and a cosmetic outfit that sold Daddy Grace Cold Cream. The article also declared that he barely escaped conviction for income tax evasion and violation of the Mann Act.

185. **"District Acts to Claim Tax on Grace's Realty,"** *Washington Post,* **May 3, 1960, p. B-2.**

The Washington, DC, Government sought a district court ruling declaring that Daddy Grace was officially domiciled in Washington. If the district government was granted such a ruling, it would get first crack at the $758,854 in real estate and inheritance taxes officials declared Bishop Grace's estate would have to pay to the local government. Federal officials, however, asserted that Grace owed nearly $6 million in back income taxes.

186. **"Dollar Bills Wave Greeting to Daddy Grace,"** *Charlotte News,* **September 7, 1956, p. B1.**

It was pointed out that Daddy Grace was in Charlotte visiting the United House of Prayer on South McDowell Street. The reporter stated that Grace's followers filled the church and danced until they were exhausted to the frenzied sound of a pumping trombone section and shouted their love for Daddy Grace——while showering him with money. A line of "angels," complete with wings, came down the middle aisle through a rose trellis covered with dollar bills, concluded the writer.

187. **Dunnigan, Alice A. "Is Daddy Grace Married?,"** *Pittsburgh Courier,* **January 4, 1958, p. 2.**

Mrs. Louvenia A. Royster, a school teacher from Georgia sued Daddy Grace for support for herself and a 30-year-old daughter. She alleged that C. M. Grace went under the name John Royster and they were married in New York on December 26, 1923. The trial for the suit was held in Washington, DC.

188. **_____. "Daddy Grace! Does He Really Have Two Wives?,"** *Pittsburgh Courier,* **January 18, 1958, p. 3, 5.**

Daddy Grace claimed that he never heard of Louvenia Hendry-Royster, the woman he is alleged to have married in 1923. His alleged daughter, Mrs. Kay Frances Anderson, stated she first met her father, C. M. Grace, when she was five years old. He was conducting a meeting in Waycross, Georgia, she said. Mrs. Anderson declared that the last time she saw him she was nineteen years old, and he asked her to travel with him. She stated that she did accompany him on a number of his ministerial tours for a short while. Mrs. Anderson declared that Daddy Grace made her stop touring with him and sent her home because she looked too much like him and his people were becoming suspicious. She also asserted that Grace warned her never to reveal her identity, and she was afraid until after she was married when her husband reminded her that this is America and nobody was going to hurt her. Several other witnesses identified Daddy Grace as John Royster, the husband of Mrs. Louvenia A. Royster. Daddy Grace denied ever marrying Mrs. Royster and stated that he was aboard a ship on his way to Jerusalem the time he was supposed to have married Mrs. Royster. During the nine days of the trial, the courtroom was packed to capacity with his followers.

189. **"Estate Case Trials Sought,"** *Standard-Times* **(New Bedford, MA), July 26, 1963, p. 4.**

Two nieces of the late Bishop Grace, Mrs. Marie J. Miller, of New Bedford, Massachussetts, and Miss Louise Grace of Osterville, Massachusetts, sued his estate for over $50,000. Mrs. Miller asked for $45,809 for numerous services and expenditures that she rendered during Grace's life. Some of the services she rendered included landscaping, charitable contributions, laundry, hospital and doctor bills and groceries. Miss Grace sued Grace's estate for $8,155. She claimed that she held a bankbook of the Philadelphia Saving Fund Society bearing the name of "Bishop" Grace with deposits in trust for her. Miss Grace also alleged that the funds in the bank were to become her property on the death of the bishop. Both nieces requested a jury trial in Superior Court in New Bedford, Massachusetts.

190. **"Evangelist Daddy Grace Dies While Visiting Los Angeles,"** *Washington Star*, **January 12, 1960, p. 1.**

This article states that Daddy Grace died in Los Angeles, California, on January 11, 1960. When Grace died, two sisters, Mrs. Sylvia Gomas and Miss Louise Grace, flew from New Bedford, Massachusetts, to take possession of his body. Mrs. Marie J. Miller of New Bedford, said, "He as just tired and worn out." She said he was 78 or 79 years old.

191. **"Fire Hose Baptism: Bishop Daddy Grace Sprinkles Followers on Harlem Street,"** *Ebony*, **Vol. 10, No. 12, October 1955, pp. 102-106.**

Daddy Grace baptized 500 almost hysterical converts with a fire hose on 115th Street in Harlem, New York. One of Grace's elders said fire-hose baptism had been part of the House of Prayer's rituals since 1933. Most of the baptism candidates ranged in age from 20 to 75 years although there were a number of children in the group. Many converts brought bottles to be filled with the water which Daddy Grace had blessed. They believed it possessed healing powers, according to the article.

192. **"Foil Daddy Grace Holdup; Church Money Guard Hurt,"** *New York Age*, **April 23, 1949, p. 1.**

Bishop Grace was visiting a local congregation in Norfolk, Virginia, and when he and his aides left the church with a sack of money, a man attempted to rob them with a gun. Bishop Grace's aides fought off the gunman. The preacher was not hurt. A similar event happened in Charlotte, NC, a few weeks earlier. The holdup was successful and money and jewels worth thousands of dollars were taken.

193. **"Followers of Daddy Grace Hold Meeting,"** *Norfolk Journal and Guide*, **October 10, 1936, p. 5.**

An estimated 2,500 followers of Daddy Grace attended the Tenth Annual House of Prayer Convention in Columbia, South Carolina. Daddy Grace attended and baptized a number of followers.

194. **Gary, Kays. "'Daddy" Will Rest in Massachusetts,"** *Charlotte Observer*, **January 13, 1960, pp. 1-2.**

Many followers of the Charlotte United House of Prayer For All People wanted Daddy Grace buried in Charlotte; however, his niece, Mrs. Marie Miller of New Bedford, Massachusetts, said he wanted to be buried in Massachusetts, "the place where he first set foot on American soil in 1903, on arrival from Portugal."

195. **Gaultney, Judy.** **"House of Prayer Got Its Start in Downtown Tent,"** *Charlotte News,* **February 17, 1979, p. B1.**

It was stated that Daddy Grace pitched a tent to hold services in Charlotte in 1926 on the corner of Third and Caldwell Streets. Crowds became so large he put up a larger tent and within about six months, Grace was forming auto caravans for baptisms at the Catawba River. Grace once explained his nickname, "Sweet Daddy," "My people call me 'Daddy' because I treat them like a father." At the House of Prayer churches, no one gets a salary and only the pastor is fully employed. There are, however, freewill offerings. These offerings are based on a Bible passage which reads, "Freely you give, freely you receive."

196. **"Grace Court Fight Impends,"** *Standard-Times* **(New Bedford, MA), April 15, 1960, p. 20.**

It was pointed out that a court battle was shaping up over the legal domicile of the late "Bishop" Charles M. Grace. The District of Columbia declared that Grace was a legal resident of that city, while the state of Massachusetts claimed he was a legal resident of that state. At stake is which municipality would get first crack at taxing the vast holdings of real and personal property of the late religious leader.

197. **"Grace Property Price to City Set at $31,718,"** *Standard-Times* **(New Bedford, MA), May 21, 1960, p. 1.**

Bishop Grace's former residence at 709 County Street was purchased by the City of New Bedford for $31,718. The city wanted the property for a new public elementary school.

198. **"Grace to Harlem,"** *Time,* **Vol. 31, No. 10, March 7, 1938, p. 30.**

It was stated that Grace purchased Father Divine's chief kingdom in Harlem, New York, for about $20,000. The writer declared that Grace's followers believed that his magazine, *The Grace Magazine,* was a "miraculous publication." Believing that this journal had power to heal, members of the cult wore copies of it strung around their necks or under their clothing, surmised the writer.

199. **"Grace's Son Files Petition,"** *Standard-Times* **(New Bedford, MA), July 12, 1962, p. 4.**

Marcellino V. Grace of Brentwood, Maryland, a son of Sweet Daddy Grace, filed a petition in probate court to contest his father's will. The son, also known as Edward Garci, was left only $2,000 in his father's will. It was also pointed out that Mrs. Jennie L. Grace, no relation to Marcellino Grace, also contested Bishop Grace's will and reportedly settled out of court for $200,000.

200. **Gubbins, Pat Borden. "Marching, Music and Memories,"** *Charlotte Observer*, **January 3, 1990, p. 1.**

This article is about Herman Coleman who is a member of the United House of Prayer For All People on Beatties Ford Road in Charlotte, North Carolina and also director of the McCullough Concert Band. Mr. Coleman recalled that his band caught the attention of Daddy Grace. Coleman's band played by ear and did not read music. Grace thought Coleman should put together a band that could read music. "Every time Bishop Grace was in town, he'd get on us to learn music, learn music," Coleman said. He continued, "He told me around September 1945, 'when I come back here, I want to see a band organized.' I had it organized in March 1946." A band of about 25 members was named for Bishop Grace. After his death in 1960, the band changed its name to McCullough Band in honor of Walter McCullough, Grace's successor.

201. **"He's Sour to Them,"** *Charlotte News*, **July 19, 1957, p. 1B.**

This article stated that Sweet Daddy Grace was having legal trouble with his neighbors. One hundred and thirty-seven of them claim his baptism services at the United House of Prayer to All People were "a shade too boisterous." Residents of the westside Detroit neighborhood in which Sweet Daddy's church was located object to services conducted over loudspeakers mounted on trucks, midnight bugle blasts, drum beating, mass hand-clapping—and firehose baptisms outside. The 78-year-old cultist was ordered to appear in court to defend himself on a nuisance charge.

202. **"House of Prayer Churches in the US,"** *The Grace Magazine*, **October 1947, p. 16.**

A number of testimonies were given in this issue as well as the addresses for forty-four United House of Prayer Churches in the United States.

203. **"House of Prayer Churches in the US,"** *The Grace Magazine*,
     November 1947, pp. 17-18.

     A number of testimonies state that Daddy Grace saved them from
     becoming sinners. This specific issue of the magazine gives the
     addresses of fifty-three House of Prayer Churches all over the United
     States.

204. **Jelton, Susan.** **"Spirit of 'Daddy Grace' Prevails,"** *Charlotte
     Observer*, **September 8, 1969, p. B1.**

     The reporter stated that the spirit of "Sweet Daddy Grace" came by to
     where it all began——the red, white and blue church building on South
     McDowell Street. It was "Emmanuel Day," climax of a week-long Holy
     Convocation at the United House of Prayer For All People. For 43
     years (since 1926), the annual "Emmanuel Day Peace Parade" drew
     thousands of persons.

205. **"Judge Ends Court Sideshow,"** *Chicago Defender*, **January 18,
     1958, p. 20.**

     The court dismissed the suit against Daddy Grace by Mrs. Louvenia
     A. Royster for child support. Mrs. Royster alleged that Grace married
     her in 1923 and fathered her child.

206. **"Judge Refuses Grace Church Receivership,"** *Washington Star*,
     April 21, 1960, p. B-2.

     Judge George L. Hart, Jr., of the District Court of Washington, DC,
     refused to put the late Bishop C. M. (Sweet Daddy) Grace's church
     into receivership. The complaint was brought by twelve members of
     the United House of Prayer For All People against Grace's successor,
     Bishop Walter McCullough. The members allege that McCullough
     was not properly elected to head the United House of Prayer For All
     People. The members, led by Rev. John W. McClure, a former
     minister of the church, sought an accounting of church funds besides
     requesting the receivership.

207. **Kilgo, John.** **"'They' Gonna Tear It Down,"** *Charlotte News*,
     December 13, 1963, p. B-1.

The United House of Prayer For All People on South McDowell Street was scheduled to be torn down to make way for redevelopment on that street. The church was built by Bishop Charles "Sweet Daddy" Grace and it was reported that this was the place where Grace preached to some of his largest and most enthusiastic congregations. It was in 1959 when Grace held his last meeting there. The people packed in to hear him. They danced and shouted and clapped their hands. Grace told them: "Daddy's people don't get in trouble. We spend our time in the House of Prayer—not in court," concluded Kilgo.

208. **"Man Who Robbed Daddy Grace Freed,"** *Charlotte Observer*, **February 23, 1950, p. B-1.**

In 1949 Clarence Jones was sentenced in Cabarrus (NC) Superior Court after he was convicted of robbing Daddy Grace of $30,000. Jones was from Charlotte. Thousands of dollars were recovered by the police. The police also recovered other items stolen from Grace, including a $1,000 platinum-cased watch; two diamond rings, one valued at $3,500; and diamond-studded keys to several safety-deposit boxes used by Daddy Grace. Jones was sentenced to four to seven years. He was paroled.

209. **McClain, Kathleen. ". . . Water from River Jordan: Baptismal Service Caps Church's Beautiful Week,"** *Charlotte Observer*, **October 8, 1990, p. A1.**

Although this article stated that more than 1,000 worshippers plunged into the outdoor baptismal pool at the "mother house" of Charlotte's United House of Prayer For All People, the writer also discussed Bishop C. M. "Sweet Daddy" Grace. Ms. McClain declared that Grace performed church services in a tent in Charlotte on Third and Caldwell streets in 1926. It was stated that the bishop led auto caravans to the Catawba River for baptisms.

210. **Miller, Hannah. "House of Prayer Bows to Progress,"** *Charlotte Observer*, **December 13, 1963, p. B1.**

The United House of Prayer For All People and a nine-room house that was the residence of Bishop Grace was scheduled to be torn down by the City of Charlotte. The House of Prayer was built by "Sweet Daddy" Grace and was the focal point of some of Charlotte's most colorful parades since it was built in 1956 at a reported cost of

$300,000, declared Ms. Miller. The writer asserted that it was here at the services the week preceding the parade, the brightly clothed bishop entered the House of Prayer each night and spoke to the faithful who pressed dollar bills upon him and broke into wild, convulsive dances.

211. **Munn, Porter. "'Daddy's' Soldiers Pay Fines," *Charlotte Observer*, February 6, 1957, p. B1.**

Seven self-styled "soldiers" of Daddy Grace paid fines in Columbia, SC, for posing as policemen and disorderly conduct. In Columbia, Gerald Dupont said he was accused of leaning against Daddy Grace's car outside the House of Prayer. He declared he was beaten by one of the "soldiers" and that when he broke away and ran, he was shot in the foot. In Charlotte, however, Police Chief Frank N. Littlejohn surmised that the uniformed and gun-toting Daddy Grace bodyguards had been regarded by police for years as being helpful in controlling crowds during visits by the religious sect leader, concluded Mr. Munn.

212. **Murphy, Harry. "State Will Settle Claim for $6,000," *Charlotte News*, July 10, 1962, p. 1.**

The State of North Carolina settled the estate of Charles M. (Sweet Daddy) Grace for $6,000. The state originally wanted $499,000 in back income taxes from the estate of Sweet Daddy. Mr. Murphy pointed out that it is difficult to tell just where Sweet Daddy ended and where his church, the United House of Prayer For All People began.

213. **"Never-Wed Teacher Says Grace," *Afro-American*, October 26, 1957, p. 1.**

Bishop Grace denied that he ever married Mrs. Louvenia A. Royster, a school teacher from Georgia who sued him for child support.

214. **"Niece, Cape Resident Sue Estate of 'Bishop' Grace," *Standard-Times* (New Bedford, MA), July 25, 1962, p. 4.**

Mrs. Marie J. Miller, a niece of Bishop Grace, sued his estate for $45,809. She claimed that was the amount due her for services that she rendered to him during his lifetime. The niece said she came to New Bedford in 1940 to care for his business matters and was told that she would be reimbursed for her expenditures and services.

According to her suit, she was never compensated for her services. Other persons also brought civil suits against Grace's estate, such as Louise Grace, another niece, and attorneys Rosalind Poll Brooker and Roy F. Teixeira.

215. **"Objectives of Printing the (Grace) Magazine,"** *The Grace Magazine*, **October 1947, p. 2.**

The Grace Magazine is the news organ of the House of Prayer For All People and was published in Philadelphia. As an agent for establishing and spreading the movement, it sets up the following objectives:

1. To unfold the hidden truth of the Gospel.

2. To magnify the life of Christ.

3. To teach to appreciate the gift of God.

4. To testify of the thousands, and healing of the millions.

216. **"Philadelphia Views Body of 'Daddy,'"** *Winston-Salem (NC) Journal*, **January 22, 1960, p. 5.**

According to this article, about 4,000 people viewed the body of Sweet Daddy Grace in Philadelphia. Some mourners refused to accept the fact that the 78-year-old leader was dead. A 19-piece band played the music of "Nearer My God to Thee" in a four-block procession to Daddy Grace's Church, the House of Prayer For All People.

217. **"Resplendent 'Daddy' Denies March to Altar,"** *Washington Star*, **January 7, 1958, p. 4.**

Daddy Grace was sued by Mrs. Louvenia A. Royster for abandoning her and her child while he was married to Royster. When his attorney asked the Bishop if he had ever married Mrs. Royster, he answered: "I swear with my hand on the Bible I never did any such thing." Grace claimed he was visiting the Near East when the marriage was supposed to have occurred. He also described himself as a poor preacher from Jerusalem. Mrs. Royster alleged that she married a man named John Royster who later used the name James Morris. She declared that Daddy Grace was the same man, James Morris.

218. **"School Site,"** *Standard-Times* **(New Bedford, MA), March 26, 1962, p. 9.**

Daddy Grace's home at 700 County Street was purchased by the City of New Bedford. The city planned to use part of the property for a new school to replace the Parker Street, Cedar Street and Merrimac Street schools.

219. **Simpson, George Eaton. "Black Pentecostalism in the United States,"** *Phylon*, **Vol. 35, No. 2, June 1974, pp. 203-211.**

The writer concludes the Daddy Grace's United House of Prayer For All People was one of the largest "deviant" groups of Black Pentecostals in the United States. Grace dominated the organization for forty years, but the church experienced a period of turbulence following his death, asserts the writer.

220. **"$600,000 Grace Title Disclosed,"** *Standard-Times* **(New Bedford, MA), July 9, 1960, p. 2.**

It was suggested that the late Bishop Charles Emmanuel Grace had title in his own name or as trustee to real estate in Los Angeles valued at approximately $600,000. Grace owned a hotel valued at $450,000. He also had titled as trustee to real estate at Berkeley Square, Los Angeles.

221. **"Socialite Files $25,000 Suit Against Daddy Grace,"** *Jet*, **April 11, 1957, p. 26.**

New York socialite Mrs. Modesta Roquemore, operator of a personal shopping service filed suit against Bishop Charles Emmanuel Grace for $25,000 for an assault upon her by one of Grace's employees, Arthur Farrington. Mr. Farrington was superintendent of a building owned by Grace realty corporation.

222. **"Special Service for 'Daddy' Tonight,"** *Standard Times* **(New Bedford, MA), January 25, 1960, pp. 1, 4.**

It was pointed out that New Bedford (MA) was the seventh and final stop for services for Daddy Grace. Several thousand people had come to New Bedford and viewed Daddy Grace's body. Services for the bishop lasted throughout the night as his body laid in a $20,000 glass-sealed casket. The body was transported to Oak Grove Cemetery in a $19,000 Cadillac hearse bought new for the funeral.

223. **Spencer, Melvin F. "Grace's Aide Cites Wide Gains,"** *Pittsburgh Courier*, **September 17, 1949, p. 13.**

The writer was an Elder in the House of Prayer, traveling aide, and companion to Bishop Grace. He called Grace's organization the "world's greatest organization." Elder Spencer stated that Grace preached the gospel in many European countries—Spain, Italy, France, England, Africa, Asia, subjected colonies, the Holy Land, and Portugal. From the outset, Bishop Grace was recognized mainly in a singular physical and spiritual essence; race, color, creed, language or nationality made little impression on his mind, according to his aide. Elder Spencer concludes: "His interest was centered on the human family, living under God."

224. **Spicer, Osker. "'An Apple a Day' May Work after All,"** *Charlotte News*, **September 16, 1982, p. B1.**

This article is mainly about Mrs. Angeline Pierce Dwiggins who said she was 107 year old. Mrs. Dwiggins regularly attends the United House of Prayer For All People on Beatties Ford Road in Charlotte—a church group she helped to establish here. She and her husband were friends of Bishop Charles "Sweet Daddy" Grace. Mrs. Dwiggins stated that Bishop Grace contributed money to help her open the Dwiggins Nursing Home in the late 1920s. She operated the facility until the early 1970s. It was later torn down during city redevelopment.

225. _____. **"The Beat Goes on for Band Tradition,"** *Charlotte News*, **December 7, 1982, pp. D1-2.**

This article is about Band Director Herman Coleman and the McCullough Band, formerly the Grace Concert Band. Mr. Coleman said his band was noticed by Bishop Grace in the late 1940s while it was playing in Charlotte. "After Bishop Grace came and heard the music, he got up and told the people that was the type of music he wanted," declared Mr. Coleman. "After that, the band was widely accepted." The original band, the Grace Concert Band, was named in Daddy Grace's honor. After Grace's death in 1960, the group's name was changed to honor Bishop Walter McCullough, who replaced Daddy Grace. The concert band, while formed at the request of Rev.

Grace, descended from a well-established musical tradition in the church, concluded Mr. Coleman.

226. **"State Reported Okaying Cut in Grace Case,"** *Winston-Salem (NC) Journal*, July 11, 1962, p. 1.

The North Carolina Department of Revenue settled the estate of Daddy Grace for $6,000. North Carolina authorities originally sought $499,000 in back income taxes from the Grace estate. This later was dropped to $109,000 and was finally settled for $6,000. The federal government sought $4.5 million from Grace's estate for back taxes, but finally settled for $1.9 million.

227. **"Suit Seeks Daddy Grace's $$,"** *Pittsburgh Courier*, May 28, 1960, p. 7.

This article asserts that Jules H. Sigal, tax consultant for the United House of Prayer For All People said Bishop Grace held close to $900,000 in his name as trustee for the church in the American Security and Trust Company, and more than $110,000 in the National Savings and Trust Company in Washington, DC. The Internal Revenue Service claimed Daddy Grace owed the government around $5.9 million and put a lien against his holdings. The writer declared that Grace is reported as having deposited more than three million dollars in the church's name in 75 banks in about 50 cities. In addition, he deposited around $500,000 in his own name, concluded the article.

228. **"Testimonials,"** *The Grace Magazine*, January 1939, pp. 2-4.

Various followers of the movement claimed that they were blessed and Bishop Grace opened their eyes to the Lord. They called him a prophet and a God-sent man. . . .

229. **"Testimonials,"** *The Grace Magazine*, January 1939, pp. 3-4.

A number of converts declared that Daddy Grace changed their whole life and that he was a man of God. Many writers stated that they were even healed of their sickness by Sweet, Sweet Daddy Grace.

230. **"Testimonials,"** *The Grace Magazine*, August 1939, pp. 3-5.

Some members of the United House of Prayer For All People testified in this magazine that Bishop Grace saved them from sin and that because of his power, their lives were turned around. They said they were grateful to him for being a man of God.

231. **"Testimonials,"** *The Grace Magazine*, **June 1940, pp. 4-5.**

The writers to this church's official organ believe that Bishop Grace helped them overcome their financial problems as well as helping them find way to the Lord. To them, Sweet Daddy Grace was wonderful.

232. **"Testimonials,"** *The Grace Magazine*, **July 1941, p. 8.**

One writer believed that Sweet Daddy Grace cured her of a disease that she had. Other writers declared that Grace had been good to them and they good for him. . . .

233. **"Testimonials,"** *The Grace Magazine*, **June 1974, p.7.**

Sister Margie Thomas of Washington, DC, stated that she had been a member of the House of Prayer for 47 years (since April 1927) and many members left during Daddy Grace's reign, but she did not take sides with those who left. She said she never doubted Bishop Grace. She was a member of the No. 2 Ushers of Charlotte (NC) Mission.

234. **"Testimonials,"** *The Grace Magazine*, **June 1974, pp. 5-10.**

Although Bishop Grace died in 1960, some of his followers continued to praise him in this magazine. Some writers claimed that Sweet Daddy Grace was God's manservant and, even though Grace was dead, his spirit was ever present in their lives.

235. **"The Daddy Grace Story,"** *New York Amsterdam News*, **September 9, 1961, p. 1.**

This article stated that Daddy Grace said he had paid $18,000,000 for a building in New York City, and, when he died, a group of New York City businessmen said Grace had agreed to sell the property to them for $5,000,000. The New York State Supreme Court denied the businessmen's contentions.

236. **"The First House of Prayer,"** *The Grace Magazine,* **April 1950, p.7.**

This magazine asserts that the first United House of Prayer For All People was established in 1919 in West Wareham, Massachusetts. It was stated that Daddy Grace constructed the first building for a total cost of thirty-nine dollars.

237. **"The House of Prayer Shall Be Established,"** *The Grace Magazine,* **October 1937, p. 8.**

An Elder Lowery gives support for the ideal of the "House of Prayer," when he declared:

> Isaiah, the son of Amos, prophesied seven hundred and twenty years before the coming of Jesus that in the last days a man would be sent from God to establish the House of Prayer For All People and the joy of the whole earth should be this house. . . .

Elder Lowery quoted other scriptures from *The Holy Bible,* to support his supposition that Daddy Grace was the man God sent to lead his people in the paths of righteousness. . . .

238. **"The Past That Haunts Daddy Grace—Dismissed Alimony Trial Reveals Secret of 1st Wife,"** *Jet,* **January 30, 1958, pp. 20-25.**

A United States District Court in Washington, DC, dismissed an alimony suit against Daddy Grace by Mrs. Louvenia A. Royster. The court said Mrs. Royster had not proven her claim that Bishop Grace had married her nor that he fathered her daughter.

239. **"Throngs in Newark Mourn Daddy Grace,"** *Winston-Salem (NC) Journal,* **January 23, 1960, p. 3.**

It was estimated that between 20,000 and 30,000 persons had viewed the body of Charles "Sweet Daddy" Grace in Newark, New Jersey. A 10-piece brass band played to the tune of "Nearer My God to Thee" in a two-block procession to Old Savoy Theater, which had been converted into the leader's church, known as The House of Prayer For All People.

240. **"20 Carolinas Bank Held Grace $$," *Charlotte Observer*, June 15, 1960, p. 1.**

This article gives a listing of the holdings in North and South Carolina of Bishop Grace as of December 31, 1956. The total amount of cash in North Carolina banks was $217, 658 (plus $330,000 in certificates of deposit at Bank of Charlotte). The total amount of cash in South Carolina banks was $10,031. He also had real estate in the Carolinas that totals $74,871, stated the reporter.

241. **"20,000 Watch Daddy Grace Parade," *Charlotte News*, September 10, 1956, p. B1.**

It was pointed out that an estimated 20,000 people lined the parade route which started at the relatively new United House For All People on South McDowell Street and wound through the Brooklyn section before returning to the same point. The writer stated that Bishop Grace sat majestically on a throne atop his float waving to his followers who shouted "hellos" to him along the line of march. The Grace Drum and Bugle Corps and other instrumental groups provided music for the marchers, but top spectator attention went to the Third Ward Shout Singers and similar groups who rode in the backs of trucks, warping tambourines against their palms to the beat of a piano in each truck.

242. **Willis, Robert A. "Body of Daddy Grace in State at Charlotte," *Winston-Salem (NC) Journal*, January 18, 1960, p. 1.**

Daddy Grace's body arrived in Charlotte, North Carolina, by train from Los Angeles. Grace's Church in Charlotte was considered the mother church he founded 34 years ago. An estimated 5,000 people viewed his remains outside the church. Mr. Willis asserts that his critics called him a charlatan. But to his poverty-stricken followers, he was not only a religious prophet—preaching a form of Christianity—but also a status symbol, concludes the reporter.

D. Articles Comparing Daddy Grace to Other Black Religious Leaders

243. **"A 'Mortal' Mystery,"** *Newsweek*, **Vol. 49, No. 23, June 10, 1957, p. 35.**

   This article was mainly about Father Divine. Father Divine had not been seen for two years. There was some speculation about his being alive. Daddy Grace said that since no one had seen Father Divine for about two years, he was most likely dead.

244. **Cooke, Mark. "'Daddy' Grace Declares War on Father Divine's 'Heaven,'"** *New York Amsterdam News*, **February 26, 1938, pp.1-3.**

   The reporter discusses Daddy Grace's purchase of Father Divine's "Heaven" in Harlem, New York. Grace paid about $22,000 for Divine's property. Many Harlemites did not want Grace to come to their community. They condemned his move on Father Divine's territory.

245. **"Daddy Grace Buys Prophet (Francis) Jones' Castle and Paints It Red, White, Blue,"** *Pittsburgh Courier*, **December 29, 1956, p. 20.**

   This article states that Daddy Grace bought Prophet Jones' Castle in Detroit and then had it painted red, white and blue. His neighbors did not like his color scheme and complained to him about the colors.

The Bishop said he liked the "blending" color. It was stated Grace
was almost a dictator and imagined himself a potentate. On one
occasion, Daddy Grace reportedly said he was born in Jerusalem. He
also said "God is my partner," and he proudly refers to the fact that
the word "Grace" is mentioned in the Bible, concludes the article.

246. **"Daddy Grace Hints Death of 'Father (Divine),'"** *Charlotte News,*
May 26, 1957, p. 1B.

It was reported that Daddy Grace, who had earlier purchased Father
Divine's holdings in New York City, said that one of best place to look
for Divine "might be in a grave." Rumors had been circulating to the
effect that Father Divine was dead. Daddy Grace said if he is alive,
no one has seen him for the past several years. "They're using
someone else for his voice and the person stays in a room away from
the audience," Daddy said.

247. **"'Daddy' Grace Invades Father Divine's Realm,"** *Journal and
Guide,* **February 26, 1938, p. 3.**

Daddy Grace purchased a five-story structure in Harlem (New York)
which had housed Father Divine's headquarters. Bishop Grace made
a $2,000 cash deposit on the property and said he would pay $20,000
more within a month. Some people in Harlem (New York) saw this
purchase simply as a move to undermine Father Divine who had
experienced several setbacks in the New York area during the past
year.

248. **"Daddy Grace Kills Time,"** *New Amsterdam News,* **June 4, 1938,
p. 2.**

Bishop Grace ordered Father Divine out of his "Kingdom" in Harlem
after he purchased it from him for $20,000.

249. **Fisher, Miles Mark. "Negroes Get Religion,"** *Opportunity,* **Vol. 14,
No. 5, May 1936, pp. 147-150.**

Dr. Fisher compares Bishop Grace to Father Divine and Elder
Solomon Lightfoot Michaux. It stated that Grace once said, "No
preacher should go to school to learn to preach." According to Rev.
Fisher, the cult leaders attempt to provide creature comforts for their
members and often extend this service to others. Bishop Grace had

a kind of hotel, where maintenance could be had for a nominal fee, connected with many Houses of Prayer. It was also stated that he had a number of small farms. Daddy Grace's church was opened to anyone and he had many white members in Charlotte, North Carolina, and other Southern towns. Bishop Grace was called "Daddy," and was the "Black Christ," and "God," to his followers, asserts the author.

250. **Higgins, Chester.   "'Sweet Daddy' Eyes a $250,000 Edifice,"** *Pittsburgh Courier*, **November 29, 1958, p. 21.**

The writer stated that Daddy Grace was in Detroit, Michigan, negotiating for the purchase of the large Tux Theatre Building for a quarter of a million dollars. Grace stated that with the purchase of this building, he would have some 400 buildings of one kind or another scattered in all parts of the world. Bishop Grace had already acquired Prophet James F. Jones' "French Castle" when Jones moved out in 1954. Daddy Grace also acquired the Prophet Jones' church, the former Oriole Theatre Building.

251. **"I Will Give Him Peace . . .,"** *Journal and Guide*, **March 12, 1938, p. 3.**

Daddy Grace presented a certified check for $18,000 to Father Divine for his headquarters in Harlem, New York. Grace had earlier paid $2,000 down on the property. Bishop Grace said of Father Divine: "I will not drive him out of Harlem. I will just let him stay. I will give him peace and pity." Retorted the Harlem Messiah: The sale left me as I shall eternally remain—well, healthy, joyful, peaceful, lively, loving, successful, prosperous, happy in spirit, body, and mind. . . . Peace, it's wonderful!"

252. **Miller, Hannah.   "The Grace and Glory Came Under Sweet Daddy's Name,"** *Charlotte Observer*, **September 10, 1982, p. 1B.**

Ms. Miller compared Bishop Walter McCullough, successor to Bishop C. M. (Sweet Daddy) Grace, to "Sweet Daddy." McCullough did not have the flamboyance of Grace. It was said that the United House of Prayer For All People can revere both Daddy Grace and Daddy McCullough. One observer argued that "Daddy (Grace) revealed his spirit in him. He does the same work and has the same power." Another observer declared:

> Daddy Grace is gone. But he sent another one to represent him. So we owe God more glory now than we did in the

presence of Bishop Grace. Because Bishop Grace has gone back to be with Father, and now we're going to produce the fruit that God desires.

253. **McClain, Kathleen. "House of Prayer Goes All Out for Convocation,"** *Charlotte Observer*, **September 29, 1990, p. 1A.**

The writer stated that the Charlotte (NC) United House of Prayer For All People planned its Sixty-Fourth Holy Convocation and that about 25,000 people were expected to attend. Ms. McClain also gave a brief sketch of Daddy Grace as well as compared him to Bishop Walter McCullough who succeeded Daddy Grace. She implied that McCullough was not as flamboyant as Grace. The writer declared that "with shoulder-length hair, a Salvador Dali mustache and curving, three-inch fingernails, Daddy Grace cut as dashing figure in flowing white robes or swallowtail coats." It was surmised that Grace was fond of parades and while attending them in Charlotte, he would sit on a throne atop a parade float and thousands of his followers would turn out a shower him with dollar bills. Bishop McCullough had gotten away from large parade and instead "has emphasized social action and self-help projects." As one follower observed: "He (McCullough) has taken us out of the storefronts and into ultramodern buildings, mortgage free." The reporter also pointed out that the United House of Prayer "Kingdom" includes about 4.5 million members in 22 states and that most of the county's 5,000 members attend the motherhouse, making it the largest congregation in the denomination as well as Charlotte's largest Black church.

254. **Perlmutt, David. "House of Prayer's Leader Dies, McCullough Ran Church 31 Years,"** *Charlotte Observer*, **March 23, 1991, p. A1.**

Although the writer discusses Bishop McCullough's death, he also compares him to Bishop Sweet Daddy Grace. Perlmutt suggests Grace was more flamboyant and his followers considered him an ambassador of Jesus Christ, a disciple blessed with the divine power to heal. The reporter concluded that Bishop McCullough was far less colorful than Daddy Grace, focusing on investing in housing for the poor and elderly and keeping young members off drugs. He also started the McCullough Scholarship for underprivileged students.

255. **_____. "Thousands Honor Late Bishop McCullough,"** *Charlotte Observer*, **March 20, 1991, p. A1.**

The writer reports on the funeral of Bishop Walter McCullough at the United House of Prayer For All People on Beattie Ford Road in Charlotte, NC. He also compares McCullough to Daddy Grace. It was stated that while Grace was flamboyant, McCullough was "a more earthly man." Bishop McCullough's followers credit him with keeping thousands of Black youths off drugs and in activities such as his well-known marching bands——which he said kept young minds from straying. One follower of McCullough declared: "He (McCullough) was not only a builder of things, but of people."

256. **"Preachers Rap Daddy Grace: Denounce Cult Leader's Move to (Harlem) Community, Purchase of (Father) Divine's Main Kingdom Draws Fire,"** *New York Amsterdam News,* **March 12, 1938, p. 1.**

The local Black ministers in Harlem, New York, denounced Daddy Grace for purchasing Father Divine's "Heaven." They considered Bishop Grace as an outsider and trying to undermine Father Divine's influence.

257. **"$200,000 Temple To Be Constructed,"** *Charlotte Observer,* **June 10, 1953, p. B-1.**

Bishop Grace purchased property in Charlotte to build a temple for his followers. It was stated that the House of Prayer in the Charlotte area had approximately 25,000 members. The Charlotte area included Concord, Mallard Creek, Gastonia, Dallas and Hickory. The building was of Spanish-type architecture and two stories high. The first floor contained an auditorium, a church cafeteria, office rooms, and other facilities. The second floor included an auditorium that would seat 1,600 persons. It should be noted that it was the policy of the House of Prayer For All People that, when a new church was being built, all of the other churches would contribute to pay for it. Hence, when the church was finished, it would be completely paid for.

258. **"'Twas Truly Wonderful (Daddy) Grace Avers,"** *New York Amsterdam News,* **June 11, 1938, pp. 1, 10.**

Daddy Grace purchased Father Divine's "Heaven" (church) in Harlem, New York. Daddy Grace declared that a new day had come to the people of Harlem and that they will no longer worship a God on earth. Bishop Grace promised that in his church, "All who believe may be saved from sin, healed from all manner of diseases, the lame may walk, the blind may see, and the evil cast out of the minds of God's children."

259. **Walker, Laurens. "He Wears Mantle of 'Daddy,'"** *Charlotte Observer*, **June 27, 1961, p. B1.**

Bishop Walter McCullough, leader of the United House of Prayer For All People and successor of the fabled C. M. (Daddy) Grace, visited Charlotte to observe "Emmanuel Day." "Emmanuel Day," the bishop explained, is celebrated by the local House of Prayer congregation in commemoration of Daddy Grace's first visit to Charlotte on June 26, 1929. The word, translated from Greek, literally means "God with us." Bishop McCullough spoke reverently of "Dad," referring to the founder of the House of Prayer, who died in Los Angeles January 12, 1960. "We regard Daddy as the same now as when he was with us in the body. The only difference is he isn't physically here." He paused, "to sort of wrap it up, you might say that the same christ that was in Daddy Grace is now in Bishop McCullough."

260. **"Who Is Biggest Showoff in Religion?,"** *Our World*, **February 1955, pp. 24-29.**

The writer stated that four men were the biggest showoff in religions: Daddy Grace, Father Divine, Prophet Jones and Elder Michaux. The author surmised that Daddy Grace was the biggest showoff of all. According to the reporter, Daddy Grace had devoted followers and he held them together with promises of healing by "Sweet Daddy." The writer contended that Grace was a "showman."

261. **"Why Daddy Grace Bought Out Prophet Jones,"** *Jet*, **May 10, 1956, pp. 22-24.**

This article stated that Daddy Grace purchased Prophet Jones' mansion in Detroit so that he would have a place to rest in comfort when he visited that city. He also wanted to make it into a show place for his followers, concluded the reporter.

IV
APPENDICES

A

Quotations and Sayings of Daddy Grace

A Selected List

"If you sin against God, Grace can save you, but if you sin against Grace, God cannot save you."

Washington Post, February 5, 1960, p. B-1

"Grace has given God a vacation, and since God is on His vacation, don't worry Him."

Washington Post, February 5, 1960, p. B-1

"Never mind about God. Salvation is by Grace only."

Washington Post, February 5, 1960, p. B-1

"Anything God offers you, I got it."

Standard-Times (New Bedford, MA), July 27, 1951, p. 4

"When I am here, God is here."

Winston-Salem (NC) Journal, January 18, 1960, p. 5

"I want everybody to know I am a good Daddy and I love all of my children."
Jet, March 23, 1957, p. 48

"I'm a Bible man from the Bible land."   "I'm preaching the last and everlasting gospel."
Winston-Salem (NC) Journal, February 14, 1957, p. 1

"Never let your left hand know what the right hand is doing."
Washington Post, March 9, 1960, p. B-1

"I give you the Bible, that's all I give you. . . ."
Winston-Salem (NC) Journal, February 14, 1957, p. 1

"I love Charlotte because I bore my cross here."
Charlotte Observer, June 19, 1959, p. B-5

"Peace, joy and comfort to you."
Winston-Salem (NC) Journal, February 14, 1957, p. 1

"I like to be near the President [of the United States]. . . . I am trying to help my people. Nobody thinks about them."
Winston-Salem (NC) Journal, January 18, 1960, p. 1

"For me, I don't care about money, I want it for you."
Winston-Salem (NC) Journal, May 4, 1952, p. 6

"Get baptized while you can. Do it this very day."
Standard-Times (New Bedford, MA), January 17, 1960, p. 3

"I try to pacify everybody."
Winston-Salem (NC) Journal, May 4, 1952

"When I come back here [Charlotte], I want to see a band organized."
Charlotte Observer, January 3, 1990, p. 1

"Clap hands for Jesus. Clap hands for God. Clap hands for the House of Prayer."

Winston-Salem **(NC)** *Journal*, **February 14, 1957, p. 1**

"No preacher should go to school to learn to preach."

Opportunity, **Vol. 14, No. 5, May 1936, p. 147**

"I'm the only poor man who doesn't charge his people a dime."

Winston-Salem **(NC)** *Journal*, **January 19, 1960, p. 1**

"We are heirs of God—saved, healed and revived. We must have the spirit to do right."

Winston-Salem **(NC)** *Journal*, **January 19, 1960, p. 1**

"Be ready, I'm leaving on the 12th to fly from Kingdom to Kingdom."

Winston-Salem **(NC)** *Sentinel*, **January 12, 1961, p. 1**

"My people call me 'Daddy' because I treat them like a father."

Charlotte News, **February 17, 1979, p. B-1**

"Daddy's people don't get in trouble. We spend our time in the House of Prayer—not in court."

Charlotte News, **December 13, 1963, p. B-1**

"I'm a servant of man."

Washington Post, **March 8, 1960, p. B-1**

"The world is coming to an end soon, and only one religion will survive."

Winston-Salem **(NC)** *Journal*, **February 14, 1957, p. 1**

"God is my partner."

Pittsburgh Courier, **December 29, 1956, p. 20**

"How can you love God when you hate those here with you . . . that's the truth unless it zig-zags on the way."

Winston-Salem **(NC)** *Journal*, **May 4, 1952, p. 6**

"The Lord saw fit to send me to America to help all those people. God was never in America until I brought him here."
Pittsburgh Courier, March 15, 1958, p. 1

"I never said I was God, but you can't prove to me I'm not."
Charlotte Observer, February 5, 1961, p. B-1

"I am just a prophet, the prophet Daniel saw in a vision."
Charlotte Observer, September 5, 1947, p. B-1

"The [my] background doesn't matter. Going forward, that is what counts."
Charlotte Observer, September 5, 1947, p. B-1

"Don't nobody try to fool me. . . . I'll knock 'em down."
Winston-Salem (NC) Journal, May 4, 1952, p. 6

"I'm not a hypocrite because I don't preach for salary. The Bible says, '. . . freely you have received, freely you give.'"
Winston-Salem (NC) Journal, January 1960, p. 12

"The God that answers by fire is the God for us to serve. . . ."
Winston-Salem (NC) Journal, May 4, 1952, p. 6

"A lot of people are stirred up . . . Why? Maybe because a lot of blankets are coming off faces because of my preaching."
Standard-Times (New Bedford, MA), July 27, 1951, p. 1

"Love of money is not the root of all evil."
Washington Post, March 9, 1960, p. B-1

"As Noah was before the flood, so is Daddy Grace before the fire."
Hue, November 1956, p. 13

"Now you see why everyone wants to say they are my wife. They see this money."
Washington (DC) Daily News, January 16, 1958, p. 18

"There's a God up there. I ought to shake the judge's hand."
New York Amsterdam News, January 25, 1958, p. 1

"They [his followers] give me their money because they know I will make it multiply for them."
Standard-Times (New Bedford, MA), March 13, 1958, p. 11

"The man who drinks shall not inherit the Kingdom of God."
New York Herald Tribune, May 11, 1958, p. 1

"If God can trust himself within me, they (his followers) can trust themselves with me."
New York Herald Tribune, May 11, 1958, p. 1

"A man's got a right to paint his house any color he wants to."
Jet, March 23, 1957, p. 47

"You don't have to be a great man. You just have to be honest."
Charlotte News, August 17, 1956, p. B-1

"I will shine my shoes on any woman I catch in the act of loving another man."
Norfolk Journal and Guide, July 11, 1936, p. 10

"Some boys came in here sick and I gave them my toast and they were well."
Charlotte Observer, June 19, 1959, p. B-5

"Don't be foolish and ignore my teaching. You can't have excuses to hide behind."
Charlotte News, August 18, 1956, p. B-1

"I am a colorless bishop."
Ebony, Vol. 8, No. 2, January 1952, p. 18

"All of our (church) meetings are conducted under the direction of the Holy Ghost."

Washington Post, March 7, 1960, p. B-1

"If they (House of Prayer Members) are hungry, I will feed them."

Jet, March 23, 1957, p. 47

"I'm happy to be with you and I'm glad to see you all."

Washington (DC) Daily News, January 16, 1958, p. 18

"I preach to all races."

Ebony, Vol. 8, No. 2, January 1952, p. 19

"It's not my little crowd against our little crowd; the House of Prayer is for ALL people."

Charlotte Observer, August 17, 1956, p. B-1

"All who believe may be saved from sin, healed from all manner of diseases, the lame may walk, the blind may see, and the evil cast out of the minds of God's children."

New York Amsterdam News, June 11, 1938, p. 1

B

Names and Titles
Given to Daddy Grace

A Selected List

"Amazing Daddy Grace"   ***Jet*, Vol. 61, No. 8, November 5, 1988, p. 37**

"Ambassador of Jesus Christ"
                    ***Charlotte Observer*, March 23, 1991, p. A-1**

"America's Richest Cultist"   ***Jet*, January 23, 1958, p. 18**

"Bishop Grace"   ***Ebony*, Vol., 8, No. 2, January 1952, p. 17**

"Bishop of the Church on the Rock"
            ***Standard-Times* (New Bedford, MA), April 27, 1941, p. 3**

"Black Christ"   ***Charlotte News*, September 11, 1938, p. 10**

"Boyfriend of the World"
            ***Newsweek*, Vol. 55, No. 7, February 15, 1960, p. 52**

"Charlatan"   ***Winston-Salem* (NC) *Journal*, January 12, 1960, p. 1**

"Daddy"   ***Washington Post*, December 21, 1957, p. A-3**

"Daddy, Sweet Daddy"
            ***Winston-Salem* (NC *Journal*, January 18, 1960, p. 5**

"Evangelist Daddy Grace"   *Washington Star*, **January 12, 1960, p. 1**

"God's Chosen One"   *Charlotte Observer*, **September 12, 1949, p. B-1**

"God's Great Man"   *Pittsburgh Courier*, **September 17, 1949, p. 13**

"God's Manservant"   *The Grace Magazine*, **June 1974, p. 5**

"God-Sent Man"   *The Grace Magazine*, **January 1939, p. 3**

"Grandiloquent Preacher"   *Life*, **Vol. 19, No. 14, October 1, 1945, p. 51**

"The Great Healer"   *The Grace Magazine*, **January 1939, p. 3**

"Greatest Humanitarian Who Ever Lived"
                    Ebony, **Vol 15, No. 6, April 1960, p. 26**

"Holder of All Keys to Heaven"
                 Newsweek, **Vol. 55, No. 7, February 15, 1960, p. 52**

"Holy Man"   *Newsweek*, **Vol. 55, No. 7, February 15, 1960, p. 52**

"Holy Prophet"   *Newsweek*, **Vol. 55, No. 7, February 15, 1960, p. 52**

"Lord Master"   *Charlotte Observer*, **September 9, 1957, p. 1**

"Man of God"   *The Grace Magazine*, **January 1939, p. 2**

"Millionaire with a Bible"   *Our World*, **Vol. 8, October 1953, p. 50**

"The Prophet"   *The Charlotte Observer*, **September 12, 1949, p. B-1**

"Showman"   *Our World*, **February 1955, p. 24**

"Sugar Daddy Grace"   *Charlotte Observer*, **September 12, 1949, p. 3**

"Sweet Daddy"   *Washington* **(DC)** *Daily News*, **January 16, 1958, p. 18**

"Sweet Daddy Grace"   *Charlotte Observer*, **June 19, 1959, p. B-5**

"Sweet Daddy, Sugar Daddy Grace"
                    Charlotte Observer, **September 12, 1949, p. 3**

"Sweet, Sweet Daddy Grace"   *The Grace Magazine*, **January 1939, p. 4**

"The Sweetest Man in the World"
                    Winston-Salem (NC) *Journal,* September 4, 1958, p. 1

"The World's Chief Cornerstone"
                    Charlotte News, August 18, 1956, p. B-1

"The World's Last Savior"   *Charlotte News,* August 18, 1956, p. B-1

C

Products Named
After Daddy Grace

A Selected List

Daddy Grace Miracle Soap
            Charlotte Observer, **September 12, 1990, p. 8**

Daddy Grace Writing Paper   *Washington Post,* **March 11, 1960, p. B-12**

Daddy Grace Tooth Paste   *Washington Post, March 11, 1960, p. B-12*

Daddy Grace Transcontinental Tea
            Winston-Salem **(NC)** *Journal,* **My 4, 1952, p. 6**

Daddy Grace Coffee   *Time,* **Vol. 75, No. 4, January 25, 1960, p. 90**

Daddy Grace Women's Pomade
            Winston-Salem **(NC)** *Journal,* **January 1960, p. 1**

Daddy Grace Face Powder
            Time, **Vol. 75, No. 4, January 25, 1960, p. 90**

All of the products were thought to have healing power and were an essential part of the spiritual exposition. Many of the products were sold at all times—even during church services

Daddy Grace Cold Water Soap
                    Charlotte Observer, September 12, 1949, p. 8

Daddy Grace Lemon Cream
                    Charlotte Observer, September 8, 1947, p. B-1

Daddy Grace Cold Cream *Time*, Vol. 75, No. 4, January 25, 1960, p. 90

Daddy Grace Eggs   *Time*, Vol. 75, No. 4, January 25, 1960, p. 90

Daddy Grace Ice Cream *Charlotte Observer*, September 5, 1947, p. B-1

Daddy Grace Pine Soap *Charlotte Observer*, September 12, 1949, p. 8

Daddy Grace Vanishing Cream
                    Washington Post, March 11, 1960, p. B-12

Daddy Grace Castile Soap
                    Charlotte Observer, September 12, 1949, p. 8

Daddy Grace Pamolive Soap *Washington Post*, March 11, 1960, p. B-12

Daddy Grace Scrumptious Cookies
                    Washington Post, March 11, 1960, p. B-12

Daddy Grace Perfume   *Charlotte Observer*, September 12, 1949, p. 8

Daddy Grace Hair Dressing *Washington Post*, March 11, 1960, p. B-12

Daddy Grace Loyal Vitamins
                    Charlotte Observer, September 5, 1947, p. B-1

Daddy Grace Lapel Buttons
                    Charlotte Observer, September 12, 1949, p. 8

D

Daddy Grace's Enterprises

A Selected List

Apartment Buildings   *Pittsburgh Courier*, May 16, 1958, p. 1

Chicken Hatchery (Cuba)   *Time*, Vol. 75, No. 4, January 25, 1960, p. 90

Coffee Plantation (Brazil)   *Time*, Vol. 75, No. 4, January 25, 1960, p. 90

Cosmetic Company   *Time*, Vol. 75, No. 4, January 25, 1960, p. 90

Factories   *Charlotte Observer*, September 12, 1949, p. 8

Farms   *Ebony*, Vol. 9, No. 1, November 1953, p. 87

Hotel   *Standard-Times* (New Bedford, MA), July 9, 1960, p. 2

Insurance Company   *Ebony*, Vol 15, No. 6, April 1960, pp. 25-26

Publishing Company   *Winston-Salem* (NC) *Journal*, May 4, 1952, p. 8

Restaurant   *Charlotte Observer*, January 19, 1960, p. 5

Soap Factory   *Charlotte Observer*, September 12, 1949, p. 8

Theaters   *Jet*, December 8, 1955, p. 21

E

Groups and Organizations Named After Daddy Grace

A Selected List

Grace Armor Bearers   *Charlotte Observer*, September 5, 1947, p. B-1

Grace Boy Scouts   *Charlotte Observer*, September 8, 1947, p. B-1

Grace Concert Band   *Charlotte News*, December 7, 1982, p. D-1

Grace Drum and Bugle Corps
                        Charlotte News, September 10, 1956, p. B-1

Grace Girl Scouts   *Charlotte Observer*, September 8, 1947, p. B-1

Grace Guards   *Charlotte Observer*, January 27, 1960, p. B-1

Grace Jubilee Choir   *Charlotte Observer*, September 8, 1947, p. B-1

Grace Just-In-Time Bombers
                        Charlotte Observer, September 8, 1947, p. B-1

---

*There was also *The Grace Magazine* (official organ of the United House of Prayer for All People), Grace Publishing Association, and Grace Foundation.

Grace Mexican Girls   *Charlotte Observer*, September 8, 1947, p. B-1

Grace Nurse Corp   *Charlotte Observer*, January 18, 1960, p. B-1

Grace Soldier   *Standard Times* (Bedford, MA), January 17, 1960, p. 8

Grace Soul Hunters   *Charlotte Observer*, September 8, 1947, p. B-1

Grace Ushers   *Charlotte Observer*, January 27, 1960, p. B-1

F

Addresses of the United House of Prayer For All People

ALABAMA

101 West 15th Street
Anniston, AL 36201

CALIFORNIA

1029 East Vernon Avenue
San Francisco, CA 90011

3125 16th Street
San Francisco, CA 94110

CONNECTICUT

1423 Straford Avenue
P. O. Box 4271
Bridgeport, CT 06607

CONNECTICUT (continued)

940 Albany Avenue
Hartford, CT 06607

11 Hazel Street
Stamford, CT 06902

100 Dixwell Avenue
New Haven, CT 06511

DELAWARE

821 East 28th Street
Wilmington, DE 19802

DISTRICT OF COLUMBIA

601 "M" Street, NW
Washington, DC 20001

---

*Additional churches may have been built since this book was published, therefore these listings may be incomplete.

DISTRICT OF COLUMBIA
(continued)

1721 1/2 Seventh Street, NW
Washington, DC 20001

1911 Sixth Street, NW
Washington, DC 20001

1123 Howard Road, SE
Washington, DC 20019

FLORIDA

4600 Northwest Second Avenue
Miami, FL 33127

2814 Northwest 22nd Avenue
Hollywood, FL 33020

2310 19th Street South
St. Petersburg, FL 33712

960 North Pearl Street
Jacksonville, FL 32102

GEORGIA

1805 Ogeechee Road
Savannah, GA 31401

160 Keener Drive
Harlem, GA 30814

1050 Quaker Road
Waynesboro, GA 30830

1101 West 45th Street
Savannah, GA 31405

Route 2, Box 80
Dearing, GA 31408

GEORGIA
(continued)

4107 Sixth Street
Savannah, GA 31408

3665 Dawn Street
Macon, GA 31204

1269 Wrightsboro Road
Augusta, GA 30901

1240 Nellieville Road
Augusta, GA 30901

P. O. Box 67
Bellville, GA 30414

1003 Echols Street
Waycross, GA 3090

1120 Pine Street
Sylvania, GA 30467

2212 Weldon Street
Savannah, GA 3140

1302 Broad Street
Claxton, GA 30417

P. O. Box 151
Guyton, GA 31312-0151

94 Mt. Zion Road
Atlanta, GA 3035

4510 Gould Street
Savannah, GA 31405

ILLINOIS

4349 South State Street
Chicago, IL 60609

INDIANA

152 East 22nd Street
Indianapolis, IN 46202

MARYLAND

600 West Preston Street
Baltimore, MD 21201

1513 Ashland Avenue
Baltimore, MD 21205

MASSACHUSETTS

337 Wilbraham Road
Springfield, MA 01190

419 Kempton Street
New Bedford, MA 02740

590 Shawnut Avenue
Boston, MA 02118

MICHIGAN

4018 Joy Road
Detroit, MI 48204

MISSOURI

5206 1/2 Page Boulevard
St. Louis, MO 63113

NEW JERSEY

1539 West Fourth Street
Piscataway, NJ 08854

NEW JERSEY (continued)

19 Kearney Avenue
Jersey City, NJ 07112

643-57 Springfield Avenue
Newark, NJ 07112

413 North Fourth Street
Vineland, NJ 08360

915 Broadway
Camden, NJ 08103

215 Graham Avenue
Paterson, NJ 07501

NEW YORK

60 Howard Street
Buffalo, NY 14206

1326 Boston Road
Bronx, NY 10456

420 Hinsdale Avenue
Brooklyn, NY 11207

2091 Amsterdam Avenue
New York, NY 10032

1381 Fulton Street
Brooklyn, NY 12216

2320 Eighth Avenue
New York, NY 10027

25 Sumpter Street
Brooklyn, NY 11233

199-15 Murdock Avenue
Hollis, LI, NY 11423

NORTH CAROLINA

2321 Beatties Ford Road
Charlotte, NC 28216

505 Holloway Street
Durham, NC 27701

2526 Statesville Avenue
Charlotte, NC 28206

P. O. Box 134
Huntersville, NC 28078

817 Cotton Grove Road
Lexington, NC 27292

P. O. Box 37435
Matthews, NC

1501 Pegram Street
Charlotte, NC 28205

7520 Cheshire Road
Derita, NC 28213

600 N. Davidson Street
P. O. Box 34413
Charlotte, NC 28202

Grace Lane
Charlotte, NC 28200

338 Sharpe Street
Mooresville, NC 28115

1019 S. Mint Street
Charlotte, NC 28203

318 Eighth Avenue Drive, SW
Hickory, NC 28601

1206 Quincy Street
Statesville, NC 28677

NORTH CAROLINA (continued)

P. O. Box 726
1209 Lawsonville Avenue
Reidsville, NC 27320

601 Beatties Ford Road
Charlotte, NC 28208

409 East South Street
Raleigh, NC 27601

101 South Dudley Street
Greensboro, NC 27401

421 East Holly Street
Dallas, NC 28034

2501 Ivy Avenue
Winston-Salem, NC 27105

908 South 13th Street
Wilmington, NC 28401

501 Old Concord Road
Salisbury, NC 28144

811 Gay Street
P. O. Box 2551
Rocky Mount, NC 27802-2551

524 Brown Street
Elizabeth City, NC 27909

501 South Mountain Street
Cherryville, NC 28021

2108 North York Street
Gastonia, NC 20852

P. O. Box 803
High Point, NC 27261-0803

253 Lincoln Street
Concord, NC 28025

OHIO

832 Fairwood Avenue
Columbus, OH 43205

8713 Cedar Avenue
Cleveland, OH 44106

3809 Woodburn Avenue
Cincinnati, OH 45207

2503 West Third Street
Dayton, OH 45408

PENNSYLVANIA

742 South 16th Street
Philadelphia, PA 19146

4033 Haverford Avenue
Philadelphia, PA 19104

349 Reilly Street
Harrisburg, PA 17102

467 West Queen Lane
Philadelphia, PA 19123

1200 North Poplar Street
Philadelphia, PA 19123

590 South First Avenue
Coatsville, PA 19320

116 East College Avenue
York, PA 17403

SOUTH CAROLINA

297 Highland Street
Spartanburg, SC 29301

P. O. Box 372
Winnsboro, SC 29180

SOUTH CAROLINA (continued)

P. O. Box 316
Anderson, SC 29621

2421 Read Street
Columbia, SC 29204

118 Gantt Street
Clemson, SC 2963

1332 Mineral Street
Greenwood, SC 29646

314 West Black Street
Rock Hill, SC 29730

31 Branch Street
Abbeville, SC 29620

315 Francis Street
Walterboro, SC 29438

General Delivery
Fairfax, SC 29827

518 Oak Street
Greer, SC 29651

709 Jenkins Street
Greenville, SC 29601

P. O. Box 594
Lancaster, SC 29720

P. O. Box 152
Tillman, SC 29943

TEXAS

4350 Kolloch Drive
Dallas, TX 75216

VIRGINIA

1811 Ivy Avenue
P. O. Box 688
Newport News, VA 23607

505 South Main Street
Norfolk, VA 23523

LaGuard Drive
Hampton, VA 23361

2715 Turnpike Road
Portsmouth, VA 23707

P. O. Box 2
South Mills, VA 27976

Index

Including authors, joint authors, and editors.
Numbers refer to entry numbers.

About the Compiler

LENWOOD G. DAVIS is professor of history at Winston-Salem State University, and the compiler of several bibliographies. He is currently working on a bibliography of Father Divine.